Devon
Edited by Donna Samworth

 Young**Writers**

First published in Great Britain in 2007 by:
Young Writers
Remus House
Coltsfoot Drive
Peterborough
PE2 9JX
Telephone: 01733 890066
Website: www.youngwriters.co.uk

SB ISBN 978-1 84602 942 4

Foreword

Young Writers was established in 1991 and has been passionately devoted to the promotion of reading and writing in children and young adults ever since. The quest continues today. Young Writers remains as committed to the nurturing of poetic and literary talent as ever.

This year's Young Writers competition has proven as vibrant and dynamic as ever and we are delighted to present a showcase of the best poetry from across the UK and in some cases overseas. Each poem has been selected from a wealth of *Little Laureates* entries before ultimately being published in this, our sixteenth primary school poetry series.

Once again, we have been supremely impressed by the overall quality of the entries we have received. The imagination, energy and creativity which has gone into each young writer's entry made choosing the poems a challenging and often difficult but ultimately hugely rewarding task - the general high standard of the work submitted ensured this opportunity to bring their poetry to a larger appreciative audience.

We sincerely hope you are pleased with this final collection and that you will enjoy *Little Laureates Devon* for many years to come.

Contents

Rowan John Williams (8)	15
Sophie Langdon (8)	15
Joseph Casey (7)	15
Joshua Westmore (8)	16
Harry Willcocks (7)	16
Ellie McCormick (7)	16
Abigail Palmer (8)	17
Mason Scott (7)	17
Angharad Smith (8)	17
Michael Watson (8)	18
Joseph Thomas (8)	18
Rhys Elliott (7)	18
Chloe Johnston (8)	19
Yasmin Sarah Gard (8)	19
James Miles (7)	19
Joshua Ryeland (7)	20
Naomi Jones (8)	20
Nathan Bookless-Browne (7)	20

Copplestone Primary School

William Wallace (9)	21
Jennifer Grey (9)	21
Jack Clarke (11)	21
Stephanie Fidock (10)	22
Stephanie Lunn (10)	23
Anju Gaston (11)	24
Joshua Hutchings (10)	24
Geordie Crozier (11)	25

Hazeldown Primary School

Holly Reed (9)	25
Annie Salter (8)	26
Callum Booker (8)	26
Anna Foster (8)	27
Charlotte Brown (8)	27
Georgia McGrane (9)	28
Shannon Ward (9)	28
Roslyn Harrion (8)	29
Aaron Scholes (8)	29
Emily Northcott (9)	30
Helena Sarah Cope (8)	30

Daniel Harvey (8)   31
Jordan Pocock (8)   31
Jazmine White (9)   32
Samuel Revell (8)   33
Paul Weatherhead (9)   33
Sophy Moyle (9)   34
Jack Phillips (9)   34
Anastasia Weston (9)   35
Matthew Brooks (9)   35
Ellen Bryan (9)   36
Sam Speed (9)   36

Horrabridge Primary School
Callum Waterhouse (8)   37
Lewis Burke (8)   37
Abigael Minns (8)   38
Rebecca Hallett (9)   39
Rebecca Luff (9)   40

Lydford Primary School
Caleb Stevens (9)   40
Thomas Sladen (7)   41
Sophie Friend (7)   41
Stephen Marsh (7)   42
Robert Heard (8)   42
Carter Davies (9)   43
Paul Sieradzki (11)   43
Elizabeth O'Neill (7)   44
Emily Friend (11)   44
Bella Westlake (8)   45
Michael Marsh (9)   45
Edward Brain (9)   46
Lauren Friend (10)   46
Jessica Harrison (8)   47
Ben Hughes (10)   47

Lympstone CE Primary School
Beth-Annie Denise Wreford (9)   48
Holly Adams (9)   48
Alice Lorna Boyes (9)   49
Katy Dallow (10)   49

Musbury Primary School

Kate Gay (7)	49
Jessica Rees (9)	50
Kayleigh Grimshaw (10)	50
Emily Gay (9)	51
Isobella Rumsby (9)	51
Rubina Jenkin (10)	52

St Peter's School, Lympstone

Rebecca Thornton (11)	52
Christian Pugsley (10)	53
Alexander Walsh (10)	53
Ben Purday	54
Alice Johnston (10)	54
Ben Pritchard (11)	55
Lyell Fuller (11)	55
Aaron Dobie (11)	56
James Potts (11)	56
Freddie House (9)	57
Andrew Brind (10)	57
Rudy Goury (11)	58
Katrina Tucker (11)	58
Vicky Anderson (11)	59
Katie Kinver (10)	59
Toby Waterworth (9)	60
Nicole Thackray (10)	60
Mabel Lai (10)	61
Harri Lai (9)	61
Megan Haward (10)	62
Maisie Pritchard (10)	62
Daniel Dobie (10)	63
George Dee-Shapland (10)	63
Sam Mason (10)	64
Thomas Packer (10)	64
Jade Broadhurst (9)	65
Olivia Young (10)	65
Barnaby Stone (9)	65
Alex Purday (9)	66
James Robert Nash Barrie (9)	66
Maximilian Savage (10)	67

Stoke Hill Junior School

Ashleigh Burns (8)	67
Martha Houston (8)	68
Jacob O'Sullivan (9)	69
Kieran Jarrett (9)	70
Brandon Green (9)	71
Rhianna Copley (9)	72
Madeleine Dugdale (8)	73
Lydia Maxted (9)	74
Reece Barett (8)	75
Jacob Warlow (9)	76
Owen Phillips (8)	77
Jordan Priddis (8)	78
Gemma Greeves (9)	79
Samuel Lemke (9)	80
Oscar Petherick (8)	81
Lauren Coles (9)	82
Oliver Bignell (8)	83
Alissa Burrows Smith (9)	84
Lottie Cornish (9)	85
Felix Holt (9)	86
Toby Crowther (9)	87
Sophia Jenkins (9)	88
Francesca Aczel (9)	89
Chloe England (8)	90
George Ford (9)	91
Tara Wood (8)	92
Freya Robertson (9)	93
Abby Carbines (9)	94
Callum Bishop (9)	95
Martha Liversedge (9)	96
Megan Hawker (8)	97
Daniel Orchard (9)	98
Aaron Hudd (9)	99
Chloe Sampson (8)	100
Elizabeth Al-Khalili (9)	101
Katie Hawes (8)	102
Alex Morgan (8)	103
Callum Oakes (9)	104
Ellie Bassett (9)	105
Amanda Herring (9)	106

Hayden Burrows (10)	128
Hanifa Nabizadeh (11)	128
Lauren Winsor (10)	129
Amy Curley (10)	129
Zoe Gould (10)	129
Joe Wakefield (11)	130
Jake Coles (10)	130
Louise Vicary (10)	130
Jai Coombes (11)	131
Nathan Henley (11)	131

The Poems

The Trust Of Others

Climbing tower,
Standing very high,
Clinging to the sturdy, old, mossy tree,
Its thousands of hands ready to hold me,
Help me, grab me, pull me up,
The millions of eyes attached
To the leafy branches of the old tree,
Watching my every move,
Waiting until my hands hurt too much
To hold on,
Straining, not wanting to let go,
But then it becomes too much.

Falling down, down, down,
Not quite ready to hit the hard, hard ground,
So scared,
I shut my eyes tight,
But then *stop!*
Not falling at all,
Just suspended in mid-air,
Swinging around,
I have the trust of others.

Kylyn Lace Hendy (11)
Boasley Cross Community School

Silver Trail

Slimy silver trail
Like a snail
Love orange peel
Plus old fruit
Most people say, *'Yuck!'*

What am I?
A slug.

Hazel Elizabeth Jeenes (9)
Boasley Cross Community School

Wicked Kennings!

I'm a . . .

Wet warrior
Shrimp muncher
Side walker
House mover
Toe nipper
Sand creeper
Mean pincher
Rock climber
Pebble cracker
Nip napper.

What am I?

A crab.

Jack William Simmons (8)
Boasley Cross Community School

Great Kennings

Salt hater
Leaf eater
Rain lover
Great climber
House carrier
Beady eyes
A spiral on the grass

What am I?

A snail.

Jasmin Dawn Pitts (8)
Boasley Cross Community School

My Kennings

Try diver
Post basher
Line out taker
Mike Catt number 12
Jamie Noon number 13
Scrum breaker
Drop kicker
Twenty-two drop out
Ollie Morgan.

What am I?

Rugby.

Luke Simmons (10)
Boasley Cross Community School

Guess What I Am?

Toy chewer
Time waster
Food eater
Teeth muncher
High jumper
Field runner
Lead walker
Cat frightener

What am I?

A dog.

Tabitha Ruth Wooldridge (10)
Boasley Cross Community School

Dartmoor

Dartmoor is a lonely place
Life up there goes at a slower pace
I am all alone up there
Just the wind blowing in my hair.

Just me and my horse
Riding through the gorse
Wind and rain, sun and snow
There is always a place to go.

Going up to Shilstone Tor
Up on top of that misty moor.
Time to turn in for the night
Make sure the bugs don't bite.

Morning has come
With a bright sun.
Today I will move on
Before the sun has gone.

The afternoon goes on
Soon the sun has gone.
Riding in the dark
Suddenly I hear a bark . . .

Then I see my dog, Rover
Now I know my journey is over.
Goodbye Dartmoor
I will be back soon!

Daisy Peters (11)
Boasley Cross Community School

My Farming - Haiku

I like Land Rovers
I like sheep an awful lot
I like fluffy lambs.

Aaron Vanstone (9)
Boasley Cross Community School

Kennings

Oval shaper
Try scorer
Scrum breaker
Line thrower

What am I?

A rugby ball.

Charlie Ogborne (9)
Boasley Cross Community School

What Am I?

I light up the night
I fill a space in your heart
If you're down, I keep you up
You cannot see me in the light
I'm very small if you look up
And I look down.

What am I?

A star.

Sean Clark (9)
Boasley Cross Community School

Kennings

An ear tipper
A meat eater
A stripe owner
A killer
A film star

What am I?

A tiger.

Pippa Hackett (9)
Boasley Cross Community School

I Want To Be A Ghost!

Sitting there, lonely in the dark,
The full moon blazing away in front of me,
While the clock chimes midnight.
My owner never took care of me,
Never wanted me in the house,
Even when I tiptoe around the house,
Scratching on the door with my claws,
With my friend, the secret mouse.
When they go out to the shops,
They lock me up in my cage,
In the freezing cold shed,
I'm starving, but I just nibble the metal on my cage,
I realise I am old, I will be buried soon.
Well, probably not, as my owners hate me,
I stop chewing
And press my face through the metal,
Suddenly, it breaks away,
I leap through the metal and onto the floor.
Then I just walk straight through the door.
I'm no longer a cat
And that's that.
I'm a ghost and well-earned too,
Because now I can do whatever I want!

Ella Creamer (9)
Boasley Cross Community School

Flowers

Snowdrops and daisy pops
Flowers are such pretty things
A pink rose that tickles your toes
Flowers have petals like the blossom on nettles
Daffodils are yellow and very mellow
Flowers' favourite season is spring,
Sometimes summer, autumn is OK
Winter is too cold.

Leah Hendy (8)
Boasley Cross Community School

The Seasons Turn

I love it when the rain's been falling
Then afterwards the robins start calling
It smells fresh of lemon and lime
In my garden at springtime

The long summer days are here to stay
The grass is greener than yesterday
The woodpecker's always pecking at my trees
And there's some honey being made by the bumblebees

The trees are the colours of red and gold
The crispy brown leaves I behold
There's a lovely little bird, oh, it's a wren
I really do love him, I've called him Big Ben

The world is a blanket of silvery lace
Although it's a blizzard, it falls with grace
I trudge through the snow in my wellington boots
I can only just hear the barn owl's hoots.

India Martin (11)
Boasley Cross Community School

The Garden

A peaceful place,
Where I can go,
To run away,
From everyone.
To hide, to seek,
To play, to sit,
To go home
At the end of every day,
Yet to come back
The very next day.

Alyse Pellow (10)
Boasley Cross Community School

Darkness

Darkness is black like a hole
Darkness sounds like someone's kicking at my wardrobe
It reminds me of a monster in my bedroom scaring me
It is like a storm in the night
Darkness tastes like an apple covered in dark chocolate
It reminds me of a black, dull roast dinner
It feels like hot, boiling lava.

Rachel Skelton (8)
Boringdon Primary School

Sadness

Sadness is blue like water
It feels like raindrops falling to the floor
It sounds like glass smashing
It reminds me of fish and chips
It is thunder and lightning sparkling
It tastes like salt water.

Luke Hill (7)
Boringdon Primary School

Anger

Anger is red like fire
It sounds like *grrrr*
It reminds me of blood
It smells like old socks
It feels like electric light
It is when the wind blows
It looks like someone cross
It tastes like red meat.

David Willing (7)
Boringdon Primary School

Happiness

Happiness is yellow like the bright sun
It sounds like a laser going through a plastic bottle
It tastes like a nice hot chocolate
It reminds me of me and my true love
Happiness is 7.30 in the morning when I fill my tummy
 The food it reminds me of, is sausages, chips and sauce
My favourite!

Esther Martin (7)
Boringdon Primary School

Laughter

Laughter is multicoloured
Laughter feels like thunder
Laughter is the school playground at lunchtime
Laughter is watching the sunset
Laughter reminds me of the park
Laughter tastes like fresh air.

Olivia Pritchard (7)
Boringdon Primary School

Sadness

Sadness is black like the dead of night
It smells like darkness
It feels like teardrops
It reminds me of thunder
It looks like grey clouds
It tastes like rotten apples.

Kieran Swatton (7)
Boringdon Primary School

Darkness

Darkness is black like chocolate
It sounds like a mouse that's lost its voice
Darkness reminds me of a haunted house
The weather is thunder and lightning storming across the sky
It looks like a blood stream with fear and terror
It feels like cold air running past
Darkness tastes like nothing but thin air
Darkness is pitch-black with coldness.

Alice Ronson (8)
Boringdon Primary School

Laughter

Laughter is brown like a bear
It tastes like chicken
It smells like a rose
It reminds me of birds' cries
It feels like the wind
It is sunny.

Nathan Willing (7)
Boringdon Primary School

Fun

It reminds me of playing football
Fun is at playtime when I can play with my friends
It looks like people laughing at jokes
It tastes like cod and chips
It reminds me of chicken burgers
Fun smells like popcorn at the cinema.

Jack Smith (8)
Boringdon Primary School

Anger

Anger is red like red rosy cheeks
It tastes like garbage
Anger is 12.00am in the morning
It feels like a giant, scaly snake or a reptile
It is a stormy sky above the sea
It sounds like a lioness roaring
It looks like a big, hairy, fierce lion
It smells like sweat
It reminds me of dark chocolate, which I hate
It smells like a fire burning down the houses.

Sophie Brotherton (7)
Boringdon Primary School

Happiness

Happiness is blue like a tidal wave
It sounds like splashing water
It tastes like the sea, salty
It feels all soft and wet
It reminds me of fresh flowers
Happiness is at 3.15pm when I go home
It reminds me of a sunny day.

Daniel Richards (8)
Boringdon Primary School

Love

It reminds me of someone kissing me
Love is night-time when I'm warm in my bed
Love smells like fish and ships when I'm really hungry
It looks like someone kissing me
Love is red like a beautiful rose.

Jordan Sunderland (8)
Boringdon Primary School

Darkness

Darkness is black like a black cat strolling down the lane
It feels like nothing, but sometimes you feel the air blowing
And brushing in your face
It reminds me of dark, melt-in-your-mouth chocolate apples
It is rainy like water dripping down one by one on your head
It sounds like a fried egg, sizzling in a frying pan
It smells like clothes going everywhere
Darkness is midnight when the sun just has to hide away.

Imogen Love (7)
Boringdon Primary School

Laughter

Laughter is red like hearts
Laughter is like a sunny day
It reminds me of a growl
It reminds me of noodles
It smells like stinky feet
It sounds like lovely singing.

Jasmine Annabelle Morgan (8)
Boringdon Primary School

Laughter

Laughter is like a red dinner tray
It reminds me of funny clowns
Laughter is seven o'clock when I go to bed
It looks like the most wonderful pattern
It feels like bread dough
Laughter is my most favourite sweet.

Alex Lecointe (8)
Boringdon Primary School

Darkness

Darkness is like black stripes on a zebra
It feels like a big blob of black stuck to the sky
It looks like a dark square
It tastes like cold pancakes
It's like a pattern of stars
It sounds like the wind howling
It reminds me of plain chocolate biscuits
It starts at 7.30pm
It ends at 5pm
It reminds me of a rainy day.

Jack Pridham (8)
Boringdon Primary School

Sadness

Sadness is blue like the sea
It sounds like someone screaming
It tastes like rough chicken
It feels like rock
It reminds me of stormy weather
Sadness is 4 o'clock in the morning when I wake up
Because my sister is crying.

Owen Gannon (7)
Boringdon Primary School

Sadness

Sadness is blue like a little swimming pool
It smells like a sock pushed up your nose
It feels like a big cut on your knee
It is a raining, pouring day like tears dropping down
It reminds me of bony chicken
It sounds like a little girl crying.

Victoria Wakeham (8)
Boringdon Primary School

Sadness

Sadness is purple like butterflies
It is like pizza with too much tomato
It reminds me of fizzy drinks that pop up my nose
It smells like a skunk
It reminds me of a bee
It sounds like a beer bottle opening
It tastes like stale cake
It reminds me of oranges squirting in your face
It feels like a spot on your nose
It reminds me of itchy grass
Sadness is blue like tears.

Megan Pridham (8)
Boringdon Primary School

Darkness

Darkness is black like a haunted house
It reminds me of dark chocolate melting
Darkness is 12 o'clock midnight when fireworks go thud in the sky
It sounds like snowy owls going *tu-whit, tu-whoo*
It reminds me of street lights going on and off in the darkness
It tastes like rain spitting.

Daniel Mills (8)
Boringdon Primary School

Anger

Anger is red like the sun burning
It is thunder and lightning like somebody's house is knocked down
It tastes like boiling pork
It reminds me of a hot volcano
It feels like I'm going to burst
Anger is 11.30pm when I get nightmares.

Amy Knight (8)
Boringdon Primary School

Sadness

It sounds like thunder
It feels like stone
It tastes like roasted snails
It's dull, dark and black
It reminds me of thunder
It looks like slimy insects
It smells like a dead flower
It's raining and a storm's coming.

Rowan John Williams (8)
Boringdon Primary School

Sadness

It feels like a balloon about to burst
It sounds like thunder
Sadness is dark blue like a deep ocean
It is raining cats and dogs
It reminds me of slimy worms
It tastes like sprouts
It smells like dead flowers
It looks like an RE lesson.

Sophie Langdon (8)
Boringdon Primary School

Fear

Fear is 12 o'clock when it is dark in the sky
It reminds me of spiders in my bed
It reminds me of burnt chicken
It smells like full bins
It feels like squashy gunk
It sounds like thunder and lightning
It is falling rocks
Fear is black like a black sky.

Joseph Casey (7)
Boringdon Primary School

Sadness

The colour of sadness is blue like an ocean
The weather is like lightning
It looks like a literacy lesson
It sounds dull and gloomy
The food of sadness is like chopped onions
The smell is like thick, choking smoke
Sadness makes me feel like I want to go and hide
It reminds me of losing something in the past.

Joshua Westmore (8)
Boringdon Primary School

Fun

It reminds me of playing on the Xbox
It looks like a balloon floating in the air
It reminds me of hot dogs
It sounds like birds tweeting
It is sunny like hot lava
It feels like pancake dough
Fun is green like mint ice cream
Fun is 12 o'clock at lunchtime.

Harry Willcocks (7)
Boringdon Primary School

Fun

It looks like a meadow of beautiful flowers
It reminds me of me and my friend, Kezia
Splashing in the sparkly blue sea
It tastes like melted chocolate pudding
Fun is playtime when we're outside
It feels like squishy pancakes
It sounds like the sea rushing onto the seashore.

Ellie McCormick (7)
Boringdon Primary School

Silence

Silence reminds me of a quiet library
It is like the sun burning
It feels like thin air
It looks like a feather falling to the ground
It reminds me of squashy marshmallows
It tastes like sweet strawberries
It sounds like soft leaves floating to the ground
It smells like sour grapes
It reminds me of a chocolate fountain
Silence is white and shiny like a clear crystal.

Abigail Palmer (8)
Boringdon Primary School

Darkness

It reminds me of the bogeyman
It smells like seaweed
It reminds me of sweet potato
It feels like rough sandpaper
It sounds like a dripping cave
The colour is like a black cloud.

Mason Scott (7)
Boringdon Primary School

Laughter

It tastes like jelly wobbling on a plate
It smells like daffodils in the meadow
It feels like fluffy white clouds
It reminds me of ice cream on my plate
Laughter is red like a rose
It reminds me of a rainbow in the sky
Laughter is playtime when I am playing in a meadow
It sounds like children playing.

Angharad Smith (8)
Boringdon Primary School

Fear

It is like the dark
It is grey like a cloud
It looks like thunder and lightning
It tastes like burnt chips
It sounds like a bang
It feels gloomy and sad
It reminds me of Brussels sprouts
It is gloomy
It is as dark as a bomb shelter.

Michael Watson (8)
Boringdon Primary School

Laughter

It feels like fluffy white clouds
It looks like a huge grey elephant
Laughter is lunchtime when I am playing
It tastes like sweet apple crumble
It smells like a chocolate fountain
It sounds like leaves rustling in the trees
Laughter is yellow like the hot sun
It reminds me of sweet and sour chicken
It reminds me of going on the First Great Western train.

Joseph Thomas (8)
Boringdon Primary School

Happiness

It reminds me of dinosaur-shaped chicken nuggets
It feels like a balloon about to burst
It smells like sweet, sugary pancakes
It tastes like chocolate ice cream
It is not like an oven
It sounds like a playground full of happy children.

Rhys Elliott (7)
Boringdon Primary School

Love

It tastes like chocolate-covered strawberries
Love is pink like a huge heart
It is warm like my cosy bed
Love is the morning when I can have a lie-in
It smells like scented roses
It sounds like the singing of the birds
It looks like a bright sparkly star shining in the sky
It reminds me of sugary sweets.

Chloe Johnston (8)
Boringdon Primary School

Fear

It smells like mouldy cheese
It reminds me of a burglar stealing me in the night
Fear is at midnight when I'm well asleep
It tastes like burnt chicken
It reminds me of broccoli and Brussels sprouts
It feels like spiders crawling on me
It sounds like a ghost in my room, booing
It is dark like a gloomy cloud
Fear is black like a cave
It looks like a spooky closet.

Yasmin Sarah Gard (8)
Boringdon Primary School

Love

Love is night-time when my friends come round for a party
It is rain, like raindrops splashing on my face
It reminds me of a delicious Hawaiian pizza
It feels like Poppy, my softest leopard toy
Love is red like a fire
Love smells like mackerel, my favourite food for tea.

James Miles (7)
Boringdon Primary School

Silence

It reminds me of a quiet library
It is clouds moving slowly
It reminds me of ice cream
It looks like quiet air
It feels like a small star
It tastes like a soft banana
It sounds like a soft piece of snow
It smells like the quiet wind blowing through the trees
Silence is white like the clouds.

Joshua Ryeland (7)
Boringdon Primary School

Laughter

It feels like there is a butterfly in my tummy
It sounds like the sea at the seashore
Laughter is bright yellow like a sunflower
It reminds me of a balloon about to *pop!*
It is sunny like bubbles floating away
It tastes like birthday cake
Laughter is painting at a party
It looks like a very tall giraffe
It smells like juicy roast pork.

Naomi Jones (8)
Boringdon Primary School

Love

It feels like happiness at the beginning of the year
It looks like a big heart
It smells like chocolate
It reminds me of a piece of chocolate
It feels like a rainbow.

Nathan Bookless-Browne (7)
Boringdon Primary School

The Gushing River

A river rushes and gushes,
Forever flowing when the wind is blowing,
The river is vast and it's rippling very fast,
But not as fast as a bike;
My old friend Mike,
Once fell into the river
And it made him shiver and quiver
Like a jelly,
Then there was a rumble in his belly,
Because he was as hungry as a starving . . .
Crocodile!

William Wallace (9)
Copplestone Primary School

Monster Poem

This monster's head is like the sun,
Its face could almost blind you,
You'd think its body is so clean,
But really, it smells like dog poo.
Its legs are as hairy as a cat,
Its arms are as smooth as glass,
But if you ever looked at it,
You might not even last!

Jennifer Grey (9)
Copplestone Primary School

What Is A Puppy?

A puppy is a ball of fluff, a playful kitten
It's like a day full of everlasting fun
Adorable like a baby
Bouncy and energetic like a kangaroo
Sleepy like a dormouse.

Jack Clarke (11)
Copplestone Primary School

The Rainforest

In the rainforest it's really wet,
If you want I can bet,
It's really wet,
In the rainforest.

Wet trees,
Damp leaves,
High sky,
Raining high.

Pouring down,
In the town,
High sky,
Morning nigh.

When morning comes,
Winds will rise up,
Like the morning sun,
Winds will blow like a fast cheetah.

Gale will come in the night,
I'll warn you, it won't be a very nice sight,
Especially on the kite,
Soon the morning will come (hopefully).

When the rain comes,
Citizens will get soaking wet,
Even the net,
Or hammock.

Stephanie Fidock (10)
Copplestone Primary School

I Wish . . .

I wish I lived beneath the sea,
All the fish would play with me,
The whales would sing,
The seahorses dance,
Round and round the dolphin prance!

With jellyfish and eels I'd swim,
With starfish I'd do water gym,
I'd slide on seaweed
And explore a cave,
Any treasure I would save!

I'd sit on rocks and comb my hair
And watch the ships go here and there,
I'd ride on a turtle,
Play cards with a crab,
Life under the sea would be just fab!

But wait . . .
At night the sea is freezing cold
And sea monster tales I have been told,
The sharks would roam
And the lobsters bite,
I think I'd have an awful fright!

In the dark, piranhas hunt,
To gobble up girls is all they want,
The fish would hide
And go to bed,
I think I'll stay on land instead!

Stephanie Lunn (10)
Copplestone Primary School

The Monster

There is a monster living in my home
And everywhere it will roam,
It isn't like most creatures,
As it has some most ordinary features,
It has a nose and a mouth,
Just like you and me,
It eats normal food and watches TV,
It will read magazines
And use anti-ageing face creams,
It makes me do homework
And in the kitchen it will lurk,
It cooks all our tea,
Like an average person, you see,
Until you realise what it is,
Spinach! And it stinks!
When you say you shall not eat it,
'You can't,' you say, 'you won't,'
It will pick up the spoon
And force-feed it down your throat,
If you fall over,
In the middle of a run,
It comes and embarrasses you,
I've got a monster of a mum!

Anju Gaston (11)
Copplestone Primary School

The River

The river is a long silver snake drifting slowly onwards,
The river is a pool of joy drifting away slowly,
The river is a mysterious thing, full of unsolved mysteries,
The river is a wonderful thing, full of surprises,
The river is a pool of wisdom, full of knowledge,
The river is a pool full of fishes jumping for joy,
The river will always be a mystery waiting to be solved.

Joshua Hutchings (10)
Copplestone Primary School

Young Writers - Little Laureates Devon

Lamborghini Gallardo

A Lamborghini is fast,
It's top of the class,
It is cool,
It's faster than a bull,
It's got four wheels,
It's not made out of steel,
Carbon fibre is good,
It's lighter than wood,
That's why a Lamborghini
Is for *me!*

Geordie Crozier (11)
Copplestone Primary School

Shipwrecked

Ghost cook cooking ghostly meals
Sailors on the lookout
Seeking enemies
Fishes swimming in-between the sails
Looking for bones to eat
Looking for bones to eat

All of the crew running to the captain
Asking for a break to eat some food
Mermaids wondering why this galleon
Sank to the bottom of the sea
And why the coral and barnacles are growing
On this ship
On this ship

Down comes a diver exploring the ship
Finds no creatures, but a shark
Swimming quickly to the surface
The shark's gone, he comes down
He's seen a shadow
The shape of death
The shape of death.

Holly Reed (9)
Hazeldown Primary School

Creepy Shipwreck

It's dark and eerie under the sea,
With treasure buried in the orange sands,
Rusted anchors and rotten doors,
Clothes remain on the dusty, dirt floors,
Dark and eerie,
Dark and eerie.

Flags floating on the cold sea waves,
Salty seaweed swaying softly,
Whilst wheels spin like mad,
Sharks circle around the grim ship,
Sharks circle,
Sharks circle.

Spooky ghosts roam the decks,
With swords stuck in their fat stomachs,
Sails still sway in the cold waves,
Large, iron cannonballs roll around the floors,
Spooky ghosts,
Spooky ghosts.

Annie Salter (8)
Hazeldown Primary School

The Sea's Prisoner

Sails torn, masts snapped
Lies the broken galleon.
Squid swim in and out
In and out of the wreck.

Bones sink into the sand
But the ghosts are still there.
Gold spills out of treasure chests.
The galleon rocks as a storm starts.

Callum Booker (8)
Hazeldown Primary School

Unknown Ship

In the deep blue sea at the bottom on the sand
A big ship was lying and bubbles were rising
Up to the surface
Up to the surface.

The shiny treasure covered with sand
And all of the bones have been eaten
By all of the creatures
By all of the creatures.

The ship is covered with seaweed and creatures
The fish are searching for food
Mermaids are swimming out and in
Out and in.

Anna Foster (8)
Hazeldown Primary School

The Mystery Ship

Under the ocean floor
The mystery ship floated down under the waves
Under the waves
Under the waves

Bubbles rising up
And up and up,
Sharks crowding round
Crowding round
Crowding round

Fish wondering why
The ship is rotten and rusty
Rotten and rusty
Rotten and rusty.

Charlotte Brown (8)
Hazeldown Primary School

Shipwreck

Under the sea lies old skeletons
And a dirty, eerie shipwreck broken in two,
Barnacles and seaweed cling onto the rusty metal,
Silver treasure and gold coins waiting to be found,
Shoals of fish swimming around,
Shoals of fish swimming around.

Crabs scuttling down the ghostly hallway,
Wheels spinning by haunted skeletons,
Rusted anchor on the sandy, rough floor,
Torn black and white flags tied on tight,
Haunted skeletons walking around,
Haunted skeletons walking around.

Riggings infested with stolen jewellery,
Seas whispering gently to the creatures in the sea,
Dolphins darting in the murky waters,
Jellyfish stinging the dead bones,
Sharks hunting for prey,
Sharks hunting for prey.

Georgia McGrane (9)
Hazeldown Primary School

The Galleon

Sharks swimming round the galleon
Little fish eat the dead humans
While barnacles grow on the ship
Grow on the ship

Sailors' bones breaking in the salty sea
Swords getting rusty, the cook's still cooking
Wooden wheel still turning, crabs getting squashed
Crabs getting squashed.

Shannon Ward (9)
Hazeldown Primary School

Shipwreck

Down, down in the murky water,
A pirate ship still sails,
Where waves echo around rotting hammocks,
Captain's hat still rests on the wheel,
A hook lies in the sand,
Hook lies in the sand.

Ghostly figures walk about,
Silver bottles to their lips,
Singing an out of tune song,
Doors hanging off hinges,
Thick anchor chains,
Thick anchor chains.

Great white shark sitting in the crow's nest,
Neptune, king of the sea, picking up all bones,
Cannon hole crammed with barnacles,
Treasure box in the sand,
A swig of rum,
A swig of rum.

The tattered flag still sways,
Skulls are hidden,
Seaweed waves on the grubby decks,
Shoals of fish swim through transparent bodies,
A skull and crossbones
Skull and crossbones.

Roslyn Harrion (8)
Hazeldown Primary School

Ghostly Galleon

Galleon underwater
Sinking downwards
Where the sharks are hunting for food
And the fishes are swimming
Galleon railing covered with seaweed and coral.

Aaron Scholes (8)
Hazeldown Primary School

The Ghostly Galleon

The wreck of the galleon is as ghostly as can be
The galleon with ghosts like me!

Sailors dance with joy to the beat of the sea
The captain with his wife - dancing, dancing.

The creatures of the deep come and visit
Sharks, hammerheads, great whites, jellyfish and fish
They swim into cabins, gliding, gliding.

The galleon's turning into coral
Barnacles stick on hard
The railings are going rotten, making a new shape
Rotten, rotten.

Emily Northcott (9)
Hazeldown Primary School

The Galleon

Deep down in the cold sea,
Ghosts roam around,
Trying to find the treasure of their dreams
Fish eating the flesh of those poor sailors
Who drowned in the war.

Little creatures are stuck to the boat,
If you were there in the ship,
You wouldn't like to be there,
Sharks are guarding the ship
They don't want anyone to be there.

The little fish start to make homes
In the ship,
But you would, wouldn't you?
Treasures are hiding in the sand,
In the sand.

Helena Sarah Cope (8)
Hazeldown Primary School

The Spirit Of The Galleon

The enemies of the galleon
Search the haunted decks
But not to Davy Jones' locker
The sharks will circle you for bones
The sharks will circle you for bones

The haunted galleon is a shipwreck
The captain is just bones
Barnacles cover the galleon
Divers searching
Divers searching

The treasure, gold and bright
Divers sharing the galleon's treasure
Crabs sliding across the deck
Fish sparkling on the ship
Fish sparkling on the ship.

Daniel Harvey (8)
Hazeldown Primary School

The Ghost Galleon

The scary skeleton captain steers his ship,
As it glides through the deep, terrifying sea,
As blue, hungry sharks swim in and out of the chambers.

Rusty cannonballs roll on the wooden, creaking floor
The captain's monkey climbs the broken rigging,
Broken rigging.

Gold spills out of the treasure chest,
Rubies, diamonds and lots more,
Lots more,
Lots more.

Jordan Pocock (8)
Hazeldown Primary School

The Galleon

A galleon is at the bottom of the ocean
She is muddy and broken
She has fish weaving around her
In and out
In and out

Rusty, crumbling, breaking boat
With the anchor falling off
And masts broken
Down in the sea
Down in the sea

Flags are torn, ragged and ripped
Sails are falling off
Ropes weaving and float
At the bottom of the sea
At the bottom of the sea

The ship is rusty, turning red, then green and white
Coral all over it, yellow coral
Fish biting it, breaking it
Swimming through the wreck
Swimming through the wreck

Ships are still falling to the bottom of the ocean
It's getting scary now and the water's cold
Deep and dark and silent
Down in the sea
Down in the sea.

Jazmine White (9)
Hazeldown Primary School

The Sinking Galleon

A galleon is sinking to the bottom of the sea
Its hull is moulding away
Everything is rusting
Everything is sinking in the sand
In the sand

Dead archers are hunting fish
Davy Jones' taking sailors' souls
The cook is still cooking
The crew are still using the head
The head

Sharks move through the rigging
Fish eat the sailors' bones
Shadows lurk at night, not day
The galleon is ever sinking
Ever sinking.

Samuel Revell (8)
Hazeldown Primary School

Out At Sea

The crabs scuttle along
The mermaids giggle
The eels swim through the shipwreck
Stinging stingrays chase the dancing fish
In the deep, deep ocean
The seagulls fly above the moving waves.

Paul Weatherhead (9)
Hazeldown Primary School

The Galleon

The galleon underwater
Fish going in the broken galleon as it lies beneath the sea
Sharks and fish eat the dead that came from the galleon
From the galleon

Creepy noises coming from the galleon
Pieces of rigging in the galleon
Fish going in and out of the creepy galleon
Pieces of wood going to fall off
Going to fall off

The cream sails are getting soggy
As sharks start to chew and make holes in it
And the rope is getting nibbled at by the fish
And sea creatures
Sea creatures

The galleon is getting old and rotten
Bits fall apart and float up to the top of the sea
Rum bottles float to the top
Float to the top.

Sophy Moyle (9)
Hazeldown Primary School

Wrecked Ship

Galleon falling in the sea
The skeleton crew eating flesh
Sharks snapping at the rotten wood.

Sailors' bones breaking in the salty sea
Weapons getting rusty
Wooden wheel still moving.

Masts floating on the water
Ghostly cook still on the deck
Whales smashing the crow's nest
As they swim by.

Jack Phillips (9)
Hazeldown Primary School

The Shipwreck

Down in the depths of the sea,
A terrible shipwreck lies,
The ghost crew of the ship, haunting all over,
Creeping, scaring anything that's near,
Anything that's near.

Creatures of the sea try to make a new home,
But are too scared to enter the wrecked ship,
Sharks guarding the haunted ship,
Outside lie the shining bones,
The shining bones.

Inside the ship the treasure waits,
For the spirits to unlock it,
Fish swim around the rigging,
As the ship slowly fades away,
Slowly fades away.

Anastasia Weston (9)
Hazeldown Primary School

The Galleon

Down below the ocean,
Lies the battered galleon,
Gun ports, hull, net, the ship's wheel doesn't spin,
Sail, flag, cabin, there's a skeleton drinking rum.

Four masts, crow's nest, rocking in the waves,
Cannonballs crashing from rock to rock
Being swallowed into the depths.

Ghosts firing cannons,
Climbing up the rigging,
The fish, dead with fright,
That's the galleon's ghosts.

The figure of a mermaid falls off the wreck,
The symbols on the sails are fading,
The boat has fallen apart.

Matthew Brooks (9)
Hazeldown Primary School

Shipwreck

Down under the shining sea,
Green, glowing pirate ghosts,
Telling jokes and drinking rum,
Down at the bottom of the sea,
Bottom of the sea,
Bottom of the sea.

Treasure lying in the sand,
Just waiting to be found,
Skeletons jumping around,
Sharks eating whatever they can see,
They can see,
They can see.

Jewels and clothes buried in the sand,
Seaweed wrapping around the ship,
Crabs scuttling through the old broken windows,
The ship rusting in the salty sea,
The ship rusting,
The ship rusting.

Ellen Bryan (9)
Hazeldown Primary School

The Sunken Galleon

The sunken galleon
All rusty and old
The captain arguing with his ghostly crew,
Arguing with his ghostly crew.

Fish are nibbling their bones
Ghost men swim through the holes in the sails
In the deep sea,
The deep sea.

Barnacles stick to the boat and coral grows
Creatures, sharks, fish and more
Divers swim to see the giant wrecks,
Giant wrecks.

Sam Speed (9)
Hazeldown Primary School

A Poem On The Senses

I like to listen to . . .
The wind swaying the branches of the pine tree,
The rain pressing against the glass of the window.

I like to smell . . .
The smell of deep fried chips,
The smell of melted chocolate,
The smell of fresh paint.

I like to feel . . .
The rain, cold on my face,
The warm, salty, sunlit sea.

Callum Waterhouse (8)
Horrabridge Primary School

Poem On The Senses

I like to listen to . . .
Children playing football in the playground,
The sea crashing onto the rocks.

I like to touch . . .
My mum's nice, warm and soft hair.

I like to look at . . .
The children playing in the river,
Ducks swimming down the river,
Children fishing for fish.

I like the taste of . . .
Chocolate melting on my tongue,
Chips from the fish and chip shop.

I like to smell . . .
The flowers in the flower shop.

Lewis Burke (8)
Horrabridge Primary School

Poem On The Senses

I like to listen to . . .
Waves crashing the shore,
Birds singing happily in the summer breeze,
Trees whistling in the breeze.

I like to look at . . .
Sunsets in the evening,
The flowers blooming,
A horse in the meadow.

I like to taste . . .
Chocolate melting in my mouth,
Fudge's sweet taste,
Ice cream giving me brain freeze.

I like to touch . . .
Snow melting in my hand,
Grass itching my nose when I lie down,
Warm sand beneath my feet.

I like to smell . . .
Poppies as their fragrance smells,
Perfume's refreshing smell,
The breeze's fresh smell.

Abigael Minns (8)
Horrabridge Primary School

Senses

I like to listen to . . .
Horses galloping in the field,
Trees blowing in the wind,
The birds tweeting in their nests.

I like to look at . . .
Splashing waves upon the seashore,
Books with many, many chapters,
Rainbows with so many colours.

I like to touch . . .
Furry, soft ponies,
Raisins because they're all shrivelled up,
Pompoms, they're all fluffy.

I like to smell . . .
A rose blooming in summer,
Delicious fruit freshly picked by hand
And roast turkey.

I like to taste . . .
The flavour of the great toffee apples,
The refreshing taste of lemonade
And the lovely taste of chocolate.

Rebecca Hallett (9)
Horrabridge Primary School

I Like . . .

I like to listen to . . .
My cute guinea pigs running around their hutch,
The fish splashing in the gleaming pond,
The breeze blowing in the hot summer air.

I like to look at . . .
Horses galloping around fields and jumping over fences,
Candyfloss-pink flowers growing peacefully in the soft sand,
Soft, squishy fruit on palm trees when I go on holiday.

I like to smell . . .
Ruby-red poppies growing in the long grass,
Freshly cut lawns with lots of beautiful flowers,
Tasty chocolate fudge being baked in the oven.

I like to taste . . .
Delicious dark chocolate melting in my mouth,
Ice lollies melting down the cone on a hot summer's day,
Blackcurrant Jammie Dodgers with their sticky jam.

I like to feel . . .
The soft sand beneath my feet,
My guinea pig's fur on the palms of my hands,
Velvet rubbing against my face.

Rebecca Luff (9)
Horrabridge Primary School

My Cat

Small, black, cuddly creature
Beautiful and soft
Her green eyes are her best feature
I don't think she needs a teacher.

Quiet, fast as a flash
Running around on the ground
Sweet, happy little cat she is
Alone on her own, quickly dashes.

Caleb Stevens (9)
Lydford Primary School

Autumn

Autumn leaves fluttering together in the breeze,
The brown leaves curling in the air,
A little breeze blows,
Blowing cold winds in the autumn breeze,
All leaves fluttering on the ground in the breeze,
Brown leaves fall on the ground in the breeze,
Autumn, cold winds in the air,
The cold grey sky when it's autumn,
Autumn goes as winter comes,
The winter breeze feels like a freezer.

Thomas Sladen (7)
Lydford Primary School

My Hamster

My hamster is as white as the snow,
He is as fluffy as grass,
He likes to store all of his food,
By his fluffy bed.

My hamster is a ball of fluff,
He looks like a ball of wool,
He is as fat as a cat,
He likes biting my finger.

My hamster is little, as little as can be,
He squeaks, he smells, he plays with me,
He's scared of the cat.

Sophie Friend (7)
Lydford Primary School

Four Seasons

Winter is cold and freezing
It makes me feel like sneezing
I like to wear my woolly hat
And cuddle up to my cat.

Summer is very hot
I like to hold a cold pot
Summer is very sunny
And people are very funny.

In spring plants grow
And the leaves are yellow.

Autumn is when leaves fall on the ground
And they go swirling around.

Stephen Marsh (7)
Lydford Primary School

Early Seasons

Spring is here again
Days are longer, nights are shorter
Animals wake up from their sleep
The birds sing a song and cheep.

It's the middle of spring
Flowers begin to bloom
The sun gets warm
Flowers grow on the lawn.

Spring is going
Passing into summer
Spring has gone
And the sun shines on.

Robert Heard (8)
Lydford Primary School

Rosy The Dog

I have a dog called Rosy
She really is quite cosy
She chews my dad's slippers
And sleeps on my bed.

She's beautiful, she's cute, she's smart
She's cool, she's tough, she's fast
She's understanding, she's loving
She's caring, she's brown, she has curly fur.

She follows me around
She makes a funny sound
She sleeps on the sofa
She looks at me weirdly.

Carter Davies (9)
Lydford Primary School

Winter

Winter is white,
White as snow,
Snow is light,
Like the air.

It's very cold,
The trees are bare,
Leaves turn to mould,
Life still survives.

Under the moon,
The frost glistens,
Spring will come soon,
So will Mother Nature.

Paul Sieradzki (11)
Lydford Primary School

My Pony

My pony is called Midnight
I kiss him when I go past
His eyes are as bright as night
I love him lost in my heart.

I ride him with chaps
And riding boots
He eats hay and feed
He wears a shiny saddle and black bridle.

He is furry and soft
He doesn't mind a brush
I put a helmet on when I ride
He is as soft as a hamster.

Elizabeth O'Neill (7)
Lydford Primary School

Super Fish

My fish likes swimming up and down,
Picking stones up while he goes down,
Then he spits them out when I give him food,
But if I don't he just frowns.

My fish is slinky and swish,
He is gentle and quiet,
He blows tender bubbles while he's swimming
And he'll always be my pet.

My fish likes his tank a lot,
With green plants all around,
He has plenty of water
And plenty of toys to swim around.

Emily Friend (11)
Lydford Primary School

Wicked Pets

My dog's called Tess
She's not very fat
She loves to run and have some fun
And bark at the cat.

My cat's called Taz
He's soft to touch
He miaows a lot
And spies on the hutch.

My rabbit's called Fudge
She's the colour of beer
She is cuddly and cute
And the food chain ends here.

Bella Westlake (8)
Lydford Primary School

Marvellous Dog

My dog, Bracken, is black and white,
My dog is playful,
My dog never fights,
My dog is very cuddly.

My dog is very happy,
My dog is very fast,
My dog's ears are very floppy,
My dog is very soft.

My dog, Bracken, lies on her tummy,
My dog is soppy,
My dog thinks it is funny,
My dog is very fluffy.

Michael Marsh (9)
Lydford Primary School

My Super Dog

My dog is really cute and cuddly
And he is always there for me.
His favourite food is definitely
A giant, huge and fat bumblebee!

He is really big and lazy
And never stops sleeping.
He is really, really greedy and never stops eating,
He is very, very mucky and always enjoys a roast ducky.

He is a really big superhero,
But out of ten, he definitely thinks he's zero.
He is definitely one in a billion,
If I had to sell him, he would cost a trillion.

Edward Brain (9)
Lydford Primary School

My Pet

My pet is cute and cuddly,
She's always there for me,
I've named her after someone,
That someone is Fee.

Fee's spotty on her tail,
As well as arms and legs.
She's always on her tummy
And is off her peg.

Her favourite food is sausages,
She always likes to sleep,
But the best thing about her is,
She's always mine to keep.

Lauren Friend (10)
Lydford Primary School

My Little Pony

My pony is called Toddy
He is cute, brown and white
He has a good spirit
He gives me a kiss.

My pony is light brown
And he is fluffy
He loves to wear my crown
When you ride, you put on a bridle.

He wears a purple rug
When he goes to a show
I wear a jacket
Toddy sometimes wears a bow.

Jessica Harrison (8)
Lydford Primary School

My Dog

My dog is tall and lazy,
He's very greedy and likes to eat,
He likes to run around and he's good
And he's got great big feet!

My dog has long ears
And they're very big,
He can look cute
And he walks like a pig.

My dog will eat anything,
He can get into a mood,
He doesn't drink much,
He never chews his food!

Ben Hughes (10)
Lydford Primary School

My Mummy

She is a hyena,
Stuck in the laughing past of my life.

My mummy is a warm blanket,
Ready to wrap me up when I am cold.

She is the sunshine,
Ready to wake me up in the morning light.

She is a PC,
Ready to be played on.

She is gold,
Ready to be picked out of a mine.

Beth-Annie Denise Wreford (9)
Lympstone CE Primary School

Pirate Poem

There once was a captain called Captain Hollow,
Her pirate life was full of woe,
Most of her crew were dead,
Some of them didn't have a head.
Her ship was called the 'Blue Pearl',
Everyone on it was a girl.
She always had a necklace that was red,
She would strangle people till they bled.
One day she got drunk,
When suddenly she sunk,
'Oh no, oh no!' she cried,
But the next thing they knew, she had died.
Her crew carried on searching for the gold,
But that's another story to be told!

Holly Adams (9)
Lympstone CE Primary School

Sea

As I sail across the sea,
For days and day without any tea,
As I dig in the sand,
I accidentally cut my hand,
As I give a big frown,
My big ships begins to go down,
Then the treasure is found!

Alice Lorna Boyes (9)
Lympstone CE Primary School

My Brother

My brother is green and goes running fast,
He is thunder, always grumbling,
He is a sports car, overtaking everyone,
He is the wind practising his whistle,
He is a lunchbox, waiting for food to go into him.

Katy Dallow (10)
Lympstone CE Primary School

The Snotty, Scary Body

Her eyes are like chickens,
Her hair is as wiggly as a snake.
Her nose is as pink as a pillow.
Her hands are as thin as a pencil.
Her knees are as holey as a badger hole.
Her feet are as hairy as a buffalo's legs.

Kate Gay (7)
Musbury Primary School

Winter To Spring

Trees are bare,
Wind is cold,
Air is soft,
Snow falls slowly.

White blanket covers the ground,
Nice toasty fire in your house,
Hot chocolate, breakfast and tea,
Staying in bed all day.

Finally spring comes,
Flowers are blooming,
Trees are green,
Butterflies are here.

Jessica Rees (9)
Musbury Primary School

The Warmest Fire

An orange and pink fire was burning,
In a quiet house,
With a curled up cat raising one eye,
With an old woman watching her
Marmalade cat,
Curled up by the orange and pink fire,
There was a knock on the door,
It was her grandchildren,
Bob and Nathan,
They raced over to the cat,
They startled the cat,
The cat ran away,
So nothing to do except go away.

Kayleigh Grimshaw (10)
Musbury Primary School

The Wintertime, The Springtime

The children playing in the snow
The cows are coming inside
The children wearing bows
The sheep are grazing outside

Nice to see the animals in the shed
The calves are being born
The children snuggled up in bed
The wrapping paper being torn

The lambs are being born
The chicks are hatching
The grass is so green on the lawn
The birds are ready for matching

Nice to see the animals out
The flowers are so bright
I like to get out and about
Oh spring is such a lovely sight.

Emily Gay (9)
Musbury Primary School

The Summer, The Winter

The summer is so lovely and bright,
It makes you see your way at night.
It makes you feel cosy and warm,
Unlike a horrible wet storm.

The winter is nasty and cold,
And all the gloves and hats are sold.
You might get horrible chilblain,
And the food will run out like rain!

Isobella Rumsby (9)
Musbury Primary School

The Weather Poem

The snow is freezing like stars falling out of the sky,
The rain is damp like someone crying,
The sun is bright like the light in my room,
The wind is cold like someone blowing on me,
The thunder is a drum like my heart beating,
The lightning is a flash of light like my torch switching on and off.

Rubina Jenkin (10)
Musbury Primary School

When The Clock Strikes Thirteen

Golden fireflies turn to frosty winter robins
When the clock strikes thirteen.
Mustard-yellow daffodils turn to chalky snowdrops
When the clock strikes thirteen.
Summer fruit trees turn to frosty wire-like branches
When the clock strikes thirteen.
Scurrying field mice turn into hibernating hedgehogs
When the clock strikes thirteen.
Warm summer rain turns to wet melting snowflakes
When the clock strikes thirteen.
Glossy crested eagles turn to chilly barn owls
When the clock strikes thirteen.
Burgundy sun-dried leaves turn to cold frost-fringed foliage
When the clock strikes thirteen.
Harlequin parasols turn to heavy tarpaulins to cover the benches
When the clock strikes thirteen.
Emerald grass snakes turn to dry dead twigs on the frosty floor
When the clock strikes thirteen.
The glittering sunlight turns to milky white moonshine
When the clock strikes one, changes reverse.

Rebecca Thornton (11)
St Peter's School, Lympstone

The Clock Strikes Thirteen

When the clock strikes thirteen,
The tiny trees shrink and the old people stretch,
Rain falls but nothing gets wet.
Fountains shoot out excess water,
Scaly goldfish swim through the air.
Pink earthworms jump up and bite the oncoming birds,
Clouds let flooding moonlight light up the Earth.
The freezing frost melts boiling grass,
The beautiful green and brown leaves turn a yellowish-blue.
Rabbits start to buzz, but bees bolt around,
The bright moon meets the glowing sun in the half-light, half-dark sky,
When the clock strikes thirteen,
Strikes thirteen,
Thirteen.

Christian Pugsley (10)
St Peter's School, Lympstone

The Clock Strikes Thirteen

The minutes pass yet the sun stays out,
Fish despise of water,
Raindrops fall, yet nothing gets wet,
Chickens strut sidewards,
Frogs leap backwards,
The garden tastes of nullity and the wind is ostentatious,
Mice chase cats,
Cats chase dogs,
People are driving backwards singing 'Road hog,'
In the meantime the grey, green and gold guinea pig gave a sigh
                                        while gobbling grass,
Then the clock strikes one and all the fun is gone.

Alexander Walsh (10)
St Peter's School, Lympstone

When The Clock Strikes Thirteen

Pigs moo, cows oink,
Chickens woof, dogs cluck.
Ash trees shrink into the ground.
Rainbows shine black and white.
The pond is frozen, the fish trapped inside.
The birds flap their wings but they only fly backwards.
Shadows jump around like they have a mind of their own.
Sunbeams soak the summer leaves.
Tree roots grow out of the ground like a hand gasping for air,
Bees go beep instead of buzz.
Suddenly the clock strikes one and the garden disappears.

Ben Purday
St Peter's School, Lympstone

Thirteen O'clock

Raindrops are falling,
But still they are as dry as bone.
Even the robin is aware of the change,
As its breast has turned to yellow,
All plants that live will meet their fate,
All dead will rise again.
Even the tough rock turned into sponge.
A lush green lawn disappears into the earth,
So only dull dirt can be seen,
The leaves on trees turn to notes,
And small buds change to coins.
All ponds start to freeze over,
Although the air is balmy,
The sun and moon can both be seen,
As they combine their awesome powers.
And after the hour of thirteen o'clock,
The clock strikes one again.

Alice Johnston (10)
St Peter's School, Lympstone

The World Turns Upside Down

Frogs turn red, standing out against the green leaf,
The ant kills the predator bird,
Flowers don't snap when stamped on,
Cat jumps and lands where it started,
There are puffy clouds but no dark shadows.
Rabbits slithering around,
Worm beats up the disgusting crow,
The warm sun shines but gives off no heat sparkles,
The grandfather clock strikes thirteen and
Everything goes back to normal.

Ben Pritchard (11)
St Peter's School, Lympstone

The Clock Strikes Thirteen

Rain falling yet nothing getting wet.
Apples with no flavour, like dried up apricots.
Trees with no roots so they cannot grow.
Night is not dark but as bright as day.
Clocks ticking backwards so time is different.
Flowers drinking blackcurrant instead of water.
Rainbows with no shine in the heavenly sky.
Money growing on trees so everybody's rich with cash.
Flies eating spiders in massive sticky webs.
Grass is red like blood has stained it.
But when the clock strikes one everything goes back to normal.

Lyell Fuller (11)
St Peter's School, Lympstone

The Clock Strikes Thirteen

Bong! Bong!
Bong! The tree bends down and picks up all its leaves,
Bong! The pig has large mirror-like bumps on its back,
Then they burst, out comes two magnificent wings,
fluorescent blue in colour.
Bong! Bong! Devouring with its razor-sharp teeth
the small kitten eats a Great Dane,
Bong! Bong! The tiny mouse thunders after the shocked cat,
Bong! Bong! The water in the pond melts
like an ice cream on a hot day,
Bong! Bong! The water in the pond forces through the ice
blocking the mini waterfall,
Bong! Suddenly, all is changed, all is quiet,
Silence!

Aaron Dobie (11)
St Peter's School, Lympstone

The Clock Struck Thirteen

When the clock struck thirteen,
The fires were extinguished,
The birds fell from the sky,
The branches snapped off trees,
The animals were struck by lightning but appeared fine,
The cats lost all their hair,
The shadows were missing,
The ponds froze over in the warmth,
The leaves fell off bushes
And the stream turned to acid.

James Potts (11)
St Peter's School, Lympstone

The Mouse

How large unto the tiny mouse,
Most small objects must appear,
A mousetrap like a chopping board,
A blade of grass like a spear.

A book like an oak door,
A tree branch like a sky tower,
A rug blanket like a football stadium,
A watering can like a shower.

A melon slice like a crescent moon,
A lollipop like traffic lights,
A speck of dust like a boulder,
Black paper like the sky at night.

A cardboard box like a classroom,
A whisker like a pencil,
A tennis ball like the shining sun,
A hollow piece of cheese like an 'O'-shaped stencil.

Freddie House (9)
St Peter's School, Lympstone

The Clock Strikes Thirteen

The brown crispy leaves turn into a lovely glistening gold,
The plain white moon turns into a glittering bright red.
All of the old black flowers rise into tall beautiful roses,
All of the dull green grass changes into a strong sparkling silver.
The old husky hooch starts to speak English.
The normal red robin starts transforming into a glamorous gold bird,
The usual hands on a human start growing into fluffy white feathers.
All the misery and sadness of the world suddenly disappears,
The soaking wet droplets from the sky fall yet nothing is touched.

Andrew Brind (10)
St Peter's School, Lympstone

When The Clock Strikes Thirteen

When the clock strikes thirteen,
Rain falls yet nothing gets drenched,
The sun is boiling but the fountain turns to ice,
The flowered garden is turning to a glossy purple,
Squeaky mice are chasing brown cats,
The sun is a marble and the moon is a football,
Mighty mice are elephants and bright white dogs are little bugs,
Black cats fly and cute birds walk slowly,
The freezing weather makes you boil,
The cold wind turns flowers back to life,
Muddy rugby balls are swimming around, dogs are statues.
But when the clock strikes again, everything turns back to normal.

Rudy Goury (11)
St Peter's School, Lympstone

The Clock Strikes Thirteen

When the clock strikes thirteen . . .
Dogs turn glittery blue and cats turn shiny green,
Daffodils spring back into life during the middle of winter,
Rain falls yet nothing gets wet,
Ants grow bigger and dogs grow smaller,
The plants grow strong although it hails
The big silver moon shines bright although it's daytime,
Birds walk sideways and cats fly backwards,
The bushes can make noises but animals can't,
In the middle of the dark night sky, the beautiful glittering sun shines
                                        a powerfully strong glaze,
The animals that fly walk and the animals that walk fly,
When the clock stops striking everything goes back to normal.

Katrina Tucker (11)
St Peter's School, Lympstone

The Clock Strikes Thirteen

When the clock strikes thirteen everything turns opposite.
Tidal waves strike, still nothing is wrecked,
Cows grow wings and birds moo,
Green grass becomes pink mud.
Daffodils turn green but die suddenly,
Rain comes down but nothing gets wet,
Rainbows turn grey, but the grey clouds become different colours,
Rain becomes purple drops of paint,
Mice dash after cats,
Fish chase dogs,
Sun produces a dark world, but the moon lights up the sky,
But when the clock next strikes everything turns back to normal.

Vicky Anderson (11)
St Peter's School, Lympstone

The Clock Strikes Thirteen

Folding its glossy wings the butter squeezed itself back into his skin.
Frosty fire makes sizzling snow.
Sunrays come down yet everything gets wet.
Perfect puppies miaow and cute kittens bark.
Crinkling furiously the holly leaves fall off like rain.
The pink perfect pigs flutter by as blue boisterous butterflies
                                    are waddling by.
Raindrops shatter down, yet everything is dry.
Stumpy trees grow, polished and elegant, flowers grow baggy barks.
The bright moon makes no spooky shadows.
The rainbow reverses the colour order and violet comes first,
                                    while red is last.
Ding-dong, the clock strikes one then, it is all normal again.

Katie Kinver (10)
St Peter's School, Lympstone

The Blue Whale

How small unto the massive whale,
Most large things must seem,
An iceberg like a grain of salt,
A current like a stream.
A fish like an annoying fly,
A shark scratching and scraping like a cat,
A bit of seaweed like a blade of grass,
A manta ray like a black mat.
A little crab, a tiny ant,
A dolphin, a flying bird,
A crab shell like a golden coin,
As the whale sweeps by, unheard.

Toby Waterworth (9)
St Peter's School, Lympstone

The Elephant

How tiny to the elephant,
Most normal things appear:
Children like plastic dolls,
Metal fences like toy prison walls,
A cold pool of water like a rippling puddle,
A white pebble, like a tiny button,
A log like a brown pencil,
A camera like a black stone,
A ladybird like a red full stop.

Nicole Thackray (10)
St Peter's School, Lympstone

The Ladybird

How large unto the ladybird
Most little things look like!
A lollipop like a big treetop,
A long thin needle like a great big spike.
A loaf of bread like a double-decker bus,
A child's stocking like an elephant's trunk,
A bright yellow flower like the shining sun,
A small little pebble like a staggering hill,
A tiny little firefly like the shining moon,
A small blue rubber like a swimming pool,
A tiny pencil like a flower's stalk,
A soft brown mushroom like a scrummy chocolate ice cream.

Mabel Lai (10)
St Peter's School, Lympstone

The Bee

How large unto the tiny bee,
Most little things appear!
A stick like a gigantic tree,
A bath like sea, so clear;
A pencil lead, a master key,
A rose, a fluffy cushion,
An ant like a dog,
A birdhouse like a rich guy's mansion.
A fence like a gateway to another world,
A driveway like an airport lane,
A snail shell like a roundabout, so curled,
A forest like a thick lion's mane.

Harri Lai (9)
St Peter's School, Lympstone

The Snake

How short unto the longest snake
Most extensive things appear
A lengthy branch, a metre rule,
A sword, a short, snub, spear.

A monkey, an annoying parasite,
A pig, a short fat buffet,
A fallen tree, a comfy home,
A rock pile, a place to stay.

A river, a wet ribbon,
A bus, like a child's toy,
A barrel of a gun, a twig
The stomach of a deer, a purse of joy.

Megan Haward (10)
St Peter's School, Lympstone

The Flea

How large unto the tiny flea
Most little things look like!
A strand of hair, a tight-rope wire,
A thick pencil, a long straight pike,
A pale yellow rose, like the sun.
A piece of paper like a wooden wall.
A plain pen, a large brown stick.
A tiny piece of blu-tack, like a big blue ball.
A white switch on a wall, like a pyramid of Wenslydale,
A tasty chipolata like a fat brown snake.
A grey cassette tape like a tall cupboard.
A boring crumb of bread, a yummy chocolate cake.

Maisie Pritchard (10)
St Peter's School, Lympstone

The Bat

How large unto the little bat,
Most small things appear!
A falcon like a bullet from a gun,
A big tree like a windy roller coaster,
A house like a great mansion,
A pencil case like a small cave,
A popcorn pot like a black hole,
A bucket of water like a great wave,
A clock like a lorry wheel,
An egg like a rugby ball.

Daniel Dobie (10)
St Peter's School, Lympstone

The Mouse

How large is the world to a tiny mouse;
How would little things appear?
Would a big rock be a house
Or a pencil, a giant spear?
Would a fly be a peregrine falcon,
Swooping very near?
Would a human be a giant?
And when he's crying, a puddle be the result of his tear?
Would a shoe be a giant's footwear
Or a fire a swarm of bees
Or a stick, a mighty tree trunk?
A tuft of grass, a forest of trees?

George Dee-Shapland (10)
St Peter's School, Lympstone

The Ant

How large to the tiny ant,
Most little things appear:
A tiny cube of cheese, a block of cement,
A drop of water, a pint of beer,
A twig over a gap, a driving board,
A splinter of wood like a pen,
A piece of hair, a nasty whip,
Humans, giant army men,
A solid pea, a football,
A cumbly leaf, a rusty boat,
A kitchen, the biggest market stall,
A puppy, a hornless goat,
A fierce cat, a mighty leopard,
A tiny book, the world's Internet,
The howling wind, a scary hurricane,
An aphid, the family's pet.

Sam Mason (10)
St Peter's School, Lympstone

The Beetle

Everything seems large to the beetle,
Even most things that are little,
A cookie like a spaceship,
A pen like a bowling skittle,
A bird like a jumbo jet,
A pebble as heavy as a car,
A little raindrop as big as the sea,
A black T-shirt as large as a pit of tar,
A four-leaf clover, a palm tree,
A shiny pound coin like a star from the sky,
A person like a giant,
A bread crumb like a large apple pie.

Thomas Packer (10)
St Peter's School, Lympstone

The Elephant

How small unto the elephant
Most large things must be -
A parrot like a flying rainbow,
An apple like a pea,
A spider like a shrivelled raisin,
A bucket of water like a still glass of wine,
Birds on the elephant's back like snowballs,
Which sends shivers down your spine.

Jade Broadhurst (9)
St Peter's School, Lympstone

The Ant

Large things to the tiny ant,
Are very small to us,
Our average house, an elephant,
A loaf of bread, a massive bus,
A CD case, a king-sized house,
An ant hill like Everest,
A lettuce leaf like a sailing boat,
Getting dinner is a quest!

Olivia Young (10)
St Peter's School, Lympstone

The Rhino

How small unto the massive rhino,
Most big things would seem,
A tree like a bush waving in the wind,
A river like a stream.
A fireplace like a plastic folder,
A glass door like a table,
A firefly like a flying spark,
A snake like a cable.

Barnaby Stone (9)
St Peter's School, Lympstone

The Blue Whale

How small unto the blue whale,
Most large things appear
A ship, a mere beetle,
A fish, a little flea.
An iceberg like a pebble,
A squid, a little key,
A massive swarm of fish, a grain of sand,
The fishing bird, a little rubber band.
The current of the sea, a tiny little stream,
A huge massive rock, a tiny little pea,
An eel as big as a finger bone,
The crying of an animal, a tiny little moan.

Alex Purday (9)
St Peter's School, Lympstone

The Fish

How big unto the tiny fish
Most little things appear!
A small group of seaweed
Like a flooded forest,
A dolphin like a whale
A salmon like a shark
A pebble, a boulder
A stalagmite, a spear
A weir like a wall.

James Robert Nash Barrie (9)
St Peter's School, Lympstone

The Panther

How strange unto a panther,
Most normal things must seem,
A rhino horn like a great sharp knife,
A tree like a giant scratching pole,
A parrot like a flying ice cream,
A tortoise like a moving rock,
A golden snake like a long sunbeam,
A monkey like a jumping spider,
A hunter like a German Shepherd,
A butterfly like a leaf in the air,
A cobra like an angry leopard,
An elephant like a huge, great rock.

Maximilian Savage (10)
St Peter's School, Lympstone

The Magic Box

(Based on 'Magic Box' by Kit Wright)

I will put in the box . . .
An angel's tear
A sip of the fizziest Coke and
The sound of Big Ben.

I will put in the box . . .
A red snowflake and a black star
A beautiful shark
And a fearsome princess.

My box is fashioned from feathers and stars
With the moon on the lid and rubies in the corners
Its hinges are sweets and chocolate.

I shall swim in my box
On the waves crashing above me
Then I will take a mermaid home with me
The colour of the grass.

Ashleigh Burns (8)
Stoke Hill Junior School

Rubber Dinghy Crocodile

'For my birthday,' Billy told me,
'What I'd really like,
Is a two seat rubber dinghy,'
So I said, 'All right.'

Billy's birthday came and went,
We went to the lake,
We took the dinghy with us,
What a big mistake.

A tree log moved towards,
Its eyes as red as blood,
Billy didn't spot it,
As it squelched through the mud.

The tree log moved closer,
I watched it for a while,
It was staring straight at Billy,
On its face lay a smile.

Suddenly a gnash of teeth,
A munch, then a crunch!
The tree log then had Billy,
For his Sunday lunch.

At Billy's funeral,
Nobody made a sound,
The vicar broke the silence saying,
'Lake now out of bounds!'

Martha Houston (8)
Stoke Hill Junior School

The Magic Box

(Based on 'Magic Box' by Kit Wright)

I will put in the box . . .

The soft touch of a purring cat,
A swish from a light saber,
The taste of warm fudge covered with melted chocolate,
And the speed of a cheetah chasing its prey.

I will put in the box . . .

The cry of a baby wanting milk,
The love of a mum seeing her newborn baby,
And the warmth of a cuddle from a big brother.

I will put in the box . . .

The last number that goes on forever,
The sadness of leaving an old school,
And the happiness of making new friends.

My box is fashioned from
All of the sweets in the world,
And packed with every gift I've ever been given,
With the love of my family in the corners.

I shall fly in my box
To fudge island
Eat the chocolate tree and drink the melted chocolate
Forever.

Jacob O'Sullivan (9)
Stoke Hill Junior School

The Magic Box

(Based on 'Magic Box' by Kit Wright)

I will put in the box . . .

The sound of angels flapping their wings
The feel of a slimy snail
And a camel's lumpy humps

I will put in the box . . .

The sound of Big Ben
A scarecrow with a tummy ache
And the sound of a wave crashing on the sand

I will put in the box . . .

A fish-faced man and a man-faced shark
An Egyptian on a horse
And a cowboy on a camel

My box is fashioned from

Cardboard and metal and angels
With stars on the lid and star dust in the corners
The hinges are made of plastic

I shall . . .

Ice skate in my box
And land in the Ice Atlantic the coldest place on Earth
The colour of the moon.

Kieran Jarrett (9)
Stoke Hill Junior School

The Magic Box

(Based on 'Magic Box' by Kit Wright)

I will put in the box . . .
A tap dancer tapping around.
A rabbit moving its nose.
A little boy with a strong touch.

I will put in the box . . .
A flying ghost with a terrible screech.
A sip of the reddest wine.
A frog bouncing up and down, up and down.

I will put in the box . . .
The first ever person to say a number.
The last memory of an ancient lizard.
The sound of an ant walking around.

I will put in the box . . .
Half a sun and a moon as small as a 5p.
An amberplane.
And an airalance.

My box is fashioned from
Diamond and rings and snow,
With a snail shell on the lid and slime in the corners.
Its hinges are gold and silver.

I shall dance in my box.
I will dance on the most popular stage,
Then bow all the way down the stairs,
Throwing flowers.

Brandon Green (9)
Stoke Hill Junior School

The Magic Box

(Based on 'Magic Box' by Kit Wright)

I will put in the box . . .
A sound from a raindrop
The hop from a rabbit
The softest fur of a cat

I will put in the box . . .
A scarecrow with a beating heart
A sip of some Coca-Cola
A sight from a ship with three decks

I will put in the box . . .
The first smile of a baby
The last trick from a clown
The sound of a fairy flapping her wings

I will put in the box . . .
A red sun and a 13th month
A beautiful prince
And a handsome princess

My box is fashioned from leather and gold and silver
With stars on the lid and spoken secrets in the corners.
Its hinges are the skin of a Dalmatian.

I shall dance in my box
In the big flashing disco
The colour of the rainbow.

Rhianna Copley (9)
Stoke Hill Junior School

The Magic Box

(Based on 'Magic Box' by Kit Wright)

I will put in the box . . .

The sound of birds singing sweetly,
The fire of a colourful phoenix,
And the touch of a warm blanket.

I will put in the box . . .

The clang of a rusty tin man,
The taste of sweet watermelon,
The beating of an eagle's wings.

I will put in the box . . .

Three yellow voices spoken in Moroccan,
The first laugh of a baby,
The last breath of a great grandad.

I will put in the box . . .

The third world of space and red grass,
A chicken with stripes,
And a zebra that clucks.

My box is fashioned from

The bark of a eucalyptus tree,
And ribbons and stitches on the edges
And leaves in the corners.

I shall go in my box

To some high snowy mountains,
And ski down them.

Madeleine Dugdale (8)
Stoke Hill Junior School

The Magic Box

(Based on 'Magic Box' by Kit Wright)

I will put in the box . . .

The sound of a giant lion shaking its mane,
And the neigh of a unicorn galloping through the snow,
And the touch of a beautiful butterfly fluttering its wings.

I will put in the box . . .

An alien that dances,
The taste of the world's finest water,
And a baby elephant stampeding in the sun.

I will put in the box . . .

Four blue secrets whispered in French,
And a last touch of a lovely great grandad,
And the first words of a baby.

I will put in the box . . .

An infinity of months in a year
And a mountain that goes underground,
And a butterfly that juggles,
And a clown that has beautiful wings.

My box is fashioned from

Pink-ice gold and water that never floods,
With stars on the lid and secrets in the corners,
And eleven little stars hidden on the bottom.

I shall fly in my box
To the furthest part of the world,
And I will go to Lapland and see the sea so light blue.

Lydia Maxted (9)
Stoke Hill Junior School

The Magic Box

(Based on 'Magic Box' by Kit Wright)

I will put in the box . . .
The sound of a fast leopard,
The ugliness of an Orc,
And the soft touch of a fluffy cloud.

I will put in the box . . .
The beats of a tin man's heart,
The taste of white broccoli,
And the kick of an angry donkey.

I will put in the box . . .
Blue whispers in the night,
The glint of a person's eye,
And the laugh of a babbling baby.

I will put in my box . . .
The thousandth day of the year and a green moon,
A baby with a crown and a king with a dummy,
And a girl with a tie and a man with a tutu.

My box is fashioned from lemon juice and banana skin,
Its hinges are made from apples,
With sapphires, rubies and emeralds scattered over it.

I shall build in my box
A small house in North America,
And a huge home in Africa,
And in a tree!

Reece Barett (8)
Stoke Hill Junior School

The Magic Box

(Based on 'Magic Box' by Kit Wright)

I will put in the box . . .

The jump of a kangaroo.
The fire of a leopard,
The bottom of a boat touching the water.

I will put in the box . . .

A snow lion with a thumping heart,
A sip of the gooiest black tar,
A leaping spark from a lake.

I will put in the box . . .

Three red wishes spoken in French,
The last memory of an ancient cat,
The first day of the year.

I will put in the box . . .

A ninth season and a wire sun,
A boat going on land,
And a car going on the water.

My box is fashioned from gold and silver and bronze,
With rainbows on the lid and surprises in the corners,
Its hinges are the colours of the rainbow.

I shall walk in my box
On the path leading to the dancing beach,
Then play in the sand
The colour of the sun.

Jacob Warlow (9)
Stoke Hill Junior School

The Magic Box

(Based on 'Magic Box' by Kit Wright)

I will put in the box . . .

The sound of a booming drum,
The stripes of a tiger,
The tip of a pen touching a board.

I will put in the box . . .

A bin with tingling fingers,
A sip of the yellowest blood,
The iron man stomping up a hill.

I will put in the box . . .

The tapping sound of a laptop,
The last laugh of a baby,
The first pyramid made.

I will put in the box . . .

A red hole and a white eclipse,
A bird with arms
And a human with wings.

My box is fashioned from copper and platinum and milk chocolate,
With a slice of cheese from the moon on the lid
And friendship in the corners
And its hinges are the beaks of pterodactyls.

I shall fly in my box
Over the great humongous Earth below me
And then land on the freezing cold North Pole.

Owen Phillips (8)
Stoke Hill Junior School

The Magic Box

(Based on 'Magic Box' by Kit Wright)

I will put in the box . . .
The first ever sound from a football crowd,
The point of a rabbit's sharp tooth,
The skin of a hippopotamus.

I will put in the box . . .
A skeleton with no bones,
A sip from the biggest pond in Exeter,
The sound of the trees waving around in the wind.

I will put in the box . . .
The whistle of a bird,
The last leaf that was grown on a tree,
The first person ever born.

I will put in the box . . .
A twenty second season and a pink sun,
A rabbit with no tail;
And a person with a tail.

My box is fashioned from
Zigzags, sequins and a big yellow ruby,
With big purple waves on the lid,
The hinges are like people's joints.

I shall swim in my box
In the biggest swimming pool in my box,
Then wash ashore onto a pirate ship,
The colour of the beach.

Jordan Priddis (8)
Stoke Hill Junior School

The Magic Box

(Based on 'Magic Box' by Kit Wright)

I will put in my box . . .
The sound of angels flapping their wings
A hot blazing sun shining in the distance
A pig doing kung fu fighting

I will put in my box . . .
Goats with a shining red heart
A bit of the best piece of magic
A memory of a fairy

I will put in my box . . .
The tear of an angel and a green flamingo
A man with eight legs
And an octopus with two legs

My box is fashioned from
Angels and animals and diamonds
With hearts on the lid and trees whispering in the corners
Its hinges are a tip of a mountain

I shall swim in my box
On the iciest water ever
Then go to the bottom
The colour of a sapphire.

Gemma Greeves (9)
Stoke Hill Junior School

The Magic Box

(Based on 'Magic Box' by Kit Wright)

I will put in the box . . .
Two kittens snuggling warm
A red squirrel up a tree
The hop of a rabbit

I will put in my box . . .
The steam from a bull
The sound of the early bird
The last memory of a cuddly kitten

I will put in the box . . .
A blue sun and a purple moon
Zeus with super strength
Hercules with thunderbolts

My box is fashioned from gold, rubies and gems
With oats on the lid and diamonds in the corners
The hinges are the jaws of foxes

I shall hang-glide in my box
Off the great Mount Everest
And land on a tree in a forest
And enjoy the view.

Samuel Lemke (9)
Stoke Hill Junior School

The Magic Box

(Based on 'Magic Box' by Kit Wright)

I will put in the box . . .
The sound of a jet plane taking off
The sight of an angry cassowary
And the first cloud to move around the Earth.

I will put in the box . . .
The water of life,
The last memory of a dead king
And the first flame on the sun.

I will put in the box . . .
A horse with six legs
Healthy chocolate
And unhealthy fruit.

My box is fashioned from
My friendship and gold and bits of fur
With silver on the lid and bronze in the corners
Its hinges are made from leather.

I shall play football in my box
In my football ground with legends of the game.
Then I will land in the corner
The colour of my toy.

Oscar Petherick (8)
Stoke Hill Junior School

The Magic Box

(Based on 'Magic Box' by Kit Wright)

I will put in my box . . .
A sound of a princess' dress swirling
A wink of a big horse
A touch of an angel's tear

I will put in my box . . .
A shine of a star
The last fairy's tear
A snowman with wriggly toes

I will put in my box . . .
A blue sun and a yellow sea
A boy with lion legs
And a lion with a boy's legs

My box is fashioned from
Black cardboard and one flower on the top
With pockets in the corners and a heart in the front
The hinges are made from hearts

I shall lie and watch the stars in my box
And ride on a shooting star
Then land on a nice beach
The colour of the sun.

Lauren Coles (9)
Stoke Hill Junior School

The Magic Box

(Based on 'Magic Box' by Kit Wright)

I will put in the box . . .
The sound of a UFO landing.
The speed of a cheetah,
And the tip of a mountain touching the sky.

I will put in the box . . .
A door with walking feet,
A sip of the coolest juice in the fridge,
A jumping letter from a mailbox.

I will put in the box . . .
The last kiss of a pharaoh,
Three choirs singing in German,
And the first giggle from a baby.

I will put in the box . . .
A white sun and a black day,
A car with rabies,
And a boy with trouble starting.

My box is fashioned from ice and gold and bronze,
With dinosaur tails on the lid and surprises in the corners.
Its hinges are made from gorilla hands.

I shall drive in my box
In the raceway 5000 and win the gold cup,
Then teach little children
Who would like to win.

Oliver Bignell (8)
Stoke Hill Junior School

The Magic Box

(Based on 'Magic Box' by Kit Wright)

I will put in the box . . .
The cold air touching your finger
The hop of a kangaroo,
The tip of a pen touching paper.

I will put in the box . . .
Frankenstein with a beating heart,
A sip of the finest blackberry juice,
The first star in the sky.

I will put in the box . . .
The first sound of a baby crying,
The last memory of learning how to walk,
The first star to fall.

I will put in the box . . .
A dinosaur and yesterday's dragonfly,
A witch on a black horse,
A jockey on a broomstick

My box is fashioned from sapphire and gold and topaz,
With black crystal on the lid and surprises in the corners,
Its hinges are made of a witch's finger.

I shall shop in my box
On the top floor in Next by the sea,
Then I will play on the beach,
The colour of fine gold.

Alissa Burrows Smith (9)
Stoke Hill Junior School

The Magic Box

(Based on 'Magic Box' by Kit Wright)

I will put in the box . . .
The sound of an echo blowing in the wind,
A crocodile's tongue touching a tooth,
A dragon's nostrils blowing a fiery leaf.

I will put in the box . . .
A scarf with indigestion,
A sip of the iciest water on Earth,
And some hot fireworks escaping from a display.

I will put in the box . . .
Two pink secrets spoken in Mongolian,
The last laugh of a boy,
The first snap of an alligator.

I will put in the box . . .
Eight days a week and an orange moon,
A dog with tentacles
And an octopus with a tail

My box is fashioned from
A metal only ever found in Africa,
And a chewed bamboo from a panda's mouth,
With snow on the lid and hearts in the corners,
Its hinges are made from friendship.

I shall sunbathe in my box,
In the clouds and then fall onto shore,
On a hot sandy beach,
And go to my jungle tree house,
My home.

Lottie Cornish (9)
Stoke Hill Junior School

The Magic Box

(Based on 'Magic Box' by Kit Wright)

I will put in the box . . .

The chattering sound of a toucan calling,
A red-striped tiger eating candy instead of deer,
And the touch of a cloud brushing your face.

I will put in the box . . .

A red Lego man's heart pounding faster than anything,
The taste of a cheese-coated coat!
And the pounce of a tiger hunting.

I will put in the box . . .

Ten brown whispers written in Japanese,
The high-pitched speech of a four-year-old boy,
And the nagging of a young girl.

I will put in the box . . .

A two hundredth colour in the spectrum,
And red shining clouds,
A cheese-eating shark and a man-eating mouse.

My box is fashioned from
The fluffiest froth of a wave,
The blood of a dragon floating on top,
And the hinges made of rainbow.

I shall cycle in my box
On the rockiest hills,
And the most beautiful glades of grass,
And finish this race in triumph.

Felix Holt (9)
Stoke Hill Junior School

The Magic Box

(Based on 'Magic Box' by Kit Wright)

I will put in the box . . .
The sound of a tummy rumbling,
A phoenix flapping its wings,
A spine of a brand new book.

I will put in the box . . .
A Lego man speeding in a car,
The taste of melted fudge,
The shine of a snake's skin on its body.

I will put in the box . . .
Red from the Welsh dragon on the flag,
A cough from a cold,
And a stomping run of an athlete.

I will put in the box . . .
The 80th day of the week and gold lava from a pink volcano,
A boy with pigtails,
And a girl with spiked-up hair.

My box is fashioned from bronze,
My box can change shape.

I shall explore in my box,
Through a fudge shop,
And have lots of fudge.

Toby Crowther (9)
Stoke Hill Junior School

The Magic Box

(Based on 'Magic Box' by Kit Wright)

I will put in the box . . .
The soft sound of a choir of angels,
Fire from a phoenix's tail,
And the strange feeling of the world in my hands.

I will put in the box . . .
The thinking brain of a shop window dummy,
The crunchy taste of the ring round Venus.
And the flick of a horse's tail.

I will put in the box . . .
Two indigo secrets spoken in Thai,
The second joke of a child,
And the last word of mine.

I will put in the box . . .
The fifty-third week in a year and a glass mountain,
A very long woodlouse,
And a scaly sausage dog.

My box is fashioned from rags and the gleaming rays from the sun,
There is love in the corners and delight in the hinges,
And on the lid four-leaf clovers and a horseshoe.

I shall fly in my box
With a unicorn by my side,
And land in a mythical place,
In a magic world in a wonderful universe.

Sophia Jenkins (9)
Stoke Hill Junior School

The Magic Box

(Based on 'Magic Box' by Kit Wright)

I will put in the box . . .
The tiny tip of a unicorn's horn,
The sound of seagulls crying loudly at dawn,
And the flap of Pegasus' wings.

I will put in the box . . .
A lonely feeling of a robot,
The taste of frosty dew in the morning,
And the cute stare of a baby gorilla.

I will put in the box . . .
Five red people's whispered secrets spoken in French
A first step of a toddler,
And a last smile of a great grandma.

I will put in the box . . .
The 8th day of the week and a violet moon,
An Inuit man sunbathing in Australia,
And an Australian woman fishing in the Arctic.

My box is fashioned from unicorn's magic
With pictures on the outside moving and looking at you,
And a unicorn's horn is Sellotaped to the side
which is also the key to the lock.

I shall horse ride in my box
On the rocky side of Mount Everest,
Then on Snowdon in Wales,
And walk along the beach at Exmouth
Into the gentle sunset.

Francesca Aczel (9)
Stoke Hill Junior School

The Magic Box

(Based on 'Magic Box' by Kit Wright)

I will put in the box . . .

The sound of birds singing in the trees,
The magic of a white unicorn,
And the soft touch of the fluffiest cloud.

I will put in the box . . .

The smile of a scarecrow,
The taste of chocolate melting in your mouth,
And the sparkle of a magic elf.

I will put in the box . . .

Six purple wishes spoken in German,
A swimming pool filled with chocolate,
And the first gurgles of a baby when he's born.

I will put in the box . . .

The tenth day of the week and a sun that never goes down,
A tiger with spots,
And a cheetah with stripes.

My box is fashioned from
Gold, silver and snow,
With little jewels on the outside,
And hinges are made from the branches of an oak tree.

I shall relax in my box
Resting on a beach in a beautiful island,
And watching the sun set.

Chloe England (8)
Stoke Hill Junior School

The Magic Box

(Based on 'Magic Box' by Kit Wright)

I will put in my box . . .
The swish of a blue light saber
The tip of two fingers touching a hand
Water from the bluest whale

I will put in my box . . .
A teddy with a human soul
A sip of chocolate from Charlie's factory
A witch coming out on Christmas Eve

I will put in my box . . .
The first cry from a newborn baby
The last words from my great uncle
And the first whisper in my ear

I will put in my box . . .
A laser and an eighth day
A dog with a wild roar
And a lion with a woof

My box is fashioned from steel and gold and fire
With wands on the lid and magic in the corners

I shall ski in my box on the mountains of Switzerland
Then on the littlest mountains
That are the colour of the whitest ice cube.

George Ford (9)
Stoke Hill Junior School

The Magic Box

(Based on 'Magic Box' by Kit Wright)

I will put in the box . . .
The twirling sparkle from a faraway tree,
The happy laugh of an elf,
The taste of the warmest ice cream in the world.

I will put in the box . . .
The stamping of a teddy bear running fast,
The crunchiest crisp and the creamiest yoghurt,
And the lovely noise of an elephant trumpeting.

I will put in my box . . .
Five red whispers spoken in Ugandan,
The last laugh from a dad,
And the first cry from a baby.

I will put in the box . . .
The sixteenth month
And a yellow volcano filled with strawberry milkshake,
An ant with very long legs,
And a giraffe with feelers.

My box is fashioned from clouds with a star on,
And a secret slot with lovely perfume smells.

I shall go camping in my box
I will go to beautiful panda castle to see animals.

Tara Wood (8)
Stoke Hill Junior School

The Magic Box

(Based on 'Magic Box' by Kit Wright)

I will put in the box . . .
The high-pitched bark of a little puppy dog,
The clear white colour of the unicorn skin,
The soft touch of cream when you dip your finger in the pot.

I will put in the box . . .
Jack and the Beanstalk - the giant's dinner,
The hot taste of a strong mint,
And the roar of a fierce lion.

I will put in the box . . .
Twenty blue shouts spoken in Korean,
The kick as a footballer scores the winning goal,
And cheers of a crowd at a rugby game.

I will put in the box . . .
The tenth day of the week and a river going up hill,
A tiger that has spots,
And a cheetah with stripes.

My box is fashioned from ice cream and chocolate,
With hearts in the corners,
And stars on the lid.

I shall surf in my box
On the beaches in India.
And catch the crashes and bangs of a storm
and trap them forever.

Freya Robertson (9)
Stoke Hill Junior School

The Magic Box

(Based on 'Magic Box' by Kit Wright)

I will put in the box . . .
The loudest noise of a grumpy elephant,
The sweetness of a pretty elf,
And the lick of a stripy tiger on my finger.

I will put into the box . . .
The waddling of a sweet penguin,
The sugary taste of sweets,
And the quiet squeak of a white mouse.

I will put into the box . . .
The red whiskers of an old Chinese man,
The cheeky laugh of a baby,
And the last prayer of an old lady.

I will put into the box . . .
The sound of the black wind in the 16th month,
A person flying really fast,
And a bird running really slow.

My box is fashioned from
Dazzling gold strips of rubies and every colour on the side,
And flowers and diamonds on the front.

I shall travel in my box
To the wilds of Africa,
And go on safari,
To see the loudest lion in the world.

Abby Carbines (9)
Stoke Hill Junior School

The Magic Box

(Based on 'Magic Box' by Kit Wright)

I will put in my box . . .

The first goal of Paul Scholes
The first sound of a newborn baby
The tip of a hand touching an arm

I will put in my box . . .

A big dinosaur with an electric tail
A sip of the coldest ice cube
David Beckham with a big tail and a dragon with football skills

I will put in my box . . .
The whistle of the blowing wind
The last save of David Seaman
And the last smile of a newborn baby

I will put in the box . . .
A talking PS2 and a hopping knife
Paul Kendrick and
Brian London

My box is fashioned from crystals and ice and gold
With clouds on the lid and roses in the corners
Its hinges are the toe joints of dinosaurs.

I shall ski in my box
On the great high mountains of Canada
Then ski ashore in a 5-star hotel
Drinking hot chocolate in the warm.

Callum Bishop (9)
Stoke Hill Junior School

The Magic Box

(Based on 'Magic Box' by Kit Wright)

I will put in my box . . .

A jump from a brown kangaroo
A sting from a queen bee,
The top of a toe touching the yellow sand,

I will put in my box . . .

A teddy with a moving leg,
A sip of salt from the warmest sea in Spain,
A loud miaow from a cat's wet mouth,

I will put in my box . . .

The sound of a buzzy bee,
The last laugh of a funny clown,
The first injection from the doctors,

I will put in my box . . .

A red moon and a ten-foot high ant,
A tiger with a mane,
And a lion with stripes,

My box is fashioned from gold and black coal,
With moons and broomsticks on the lid and prayers in the corners.
Its hinges are witches' fingers.

I shall surf in my box
On the great high mountains of Canada,
Then snow plough down a white mountain,
The colour of a white tiger.

Martha Liversedge (9)
Stoke Hill Junior School

The Magic Box

(Based on 'Magic Box' by Kit Wright)

I will put in my box . . .
A pencil case with a rumbling tummy
A sip of the coldest chocolate from a fountain
A laugh from the mouth of a hyena

I will put in my box . . .
A squeaking door
The last spinning pound coin from my grandad
A cheer from the football ground

I will put in my box . . .
A cold, cold sun
A big kangaroo, which runs
And a small lion, which jumps

My box is fashioned from willow and wood
With gnomes on the lid and hedgehogs' spines in the corner
Its hinges have half a clock in each one.

I shall walk my dogs in my box
In a gigantic park in Devon
Then get dragged into a dog café by my dogs
With dirty clothes the colour of mud.

Megan Hawker (8)
Stoke Hill Junior School

The Magic Box

(Based on 'Magic Box' by Kit Wright)

I will put in my box . . .
The skating of a teenager
The sharp teeth from the mouth of a great white shark
The tip of a finger touching a toe

I will put in my box . . .
A toy with a headache
A sip of orange from the juicy fruit
A hand from a silver-back gorilla

I will put in my box . . .
A lion's great roar and a crocodile's snap
The last time I saw my grandad
And the first ride of a sports car

I will put in my box . . .
A hot ice cube and a cold fire
The cat being chased by a mouse
And the mouse being chased by a dog

My box is fashioned from dinosaurs' skin and a black dust
With two red eyes on the lid and spiders' webs in the corners
Its hinges are the gold of the brightest leprechaun

I shall have an adventure in my box
In the lost world of the jungle
I will then ride a T-rex, the colour of a dark cave.

Daniel Orchard (9)
Stoke Hill Junior School

The Magic Box

(Based on 'Magic Box' by Kit Wright)

I will put in my box . . .

The first movement of a pig
The trunk of an elephant
The tip of a finger touching a tooth

I will put in my box . . .

The Iron Man with a headache
A sip of juice from the bottle
The tiger's roar

I will put in my box . . .

The sound of baby's cry
The laugh of Colin
The first kiss from my mum

I will put in my box . . .

A talking football pitch
Rooney with a fat tummy
And Shrek with football skills

My box is fashioned from gold and plastic and grass
With thunder in the corners
And stars for the hinges

I shall play football in my box
On the great stadium of Old Trafford
Then score a goal on the grass
With light shining on the pitch.

Aaron Hudd (9)
Stoke Hill Junior School

The Magic Box

(Based on 'Magic Box' by Kit Wright)

I will put in the box . . .

A swish from a dancer in her dress
Air from the mouth of an Indian dragon
The tip of a hairbrush

I will put in the box . . .

A pencil case with a best friend
A slip of the Iron Man's earwax
A purple ogre from planet Ogled

I will put in the box . . .

A shouting memo board
The last hug from an ancient grandma
The first cry from a baby

I will put in the box . . .

A pink ogre and a blue moon
An Ellie Sampson
And a Chloe Basset

My box is fashioned with gold and ice and wood
With lightning on the lid
And dogs in the corners
Its hinges are made of stainless steel

I shall walk dogs in my box
In the biggest park in Devon
And skid to a halt in a café
The colour of a sunny day.

Chloe Sampson (8)
Stoke Hill Junior School

The Magic Box

(Based on 'Magic Box' by Kit Wright)

I will put in my box . . .

The hair of a mermaid
The stripe off a tiger's back
The tip of a finger touching a knee.

I will put in my box . . .

A house with an evil eye
A sip of the sweetest sugar
A sweet smell from a beautiful rose.

I will put in my box . . .

Three blue wishes spoken in Arabic
The last laugh of an ancient fairy
And a first shining comet in the night sky.

I will put in my box . . .

All the Seven Sisters shining in the night sky.
A cat that moos
And a cow that miaows.

My box is fashioned from
Bones of an elf and dinosaur dust
With white clouds on the lid
And whispers in the corners
And also feathers from a rainbow bird.

I shall fish in my box
And catch a giant fish
The size of an elephant
And the colour of
Fresh green grass.

Elizabeth Al-Khalili (9)
Stoke Hill Junior School

The Magic Box

(Based on 'Magic Box' by Kit Wright)

I will put in my box . . .

The bounce of a jumping dolphin
A roar from the mouth of a lion
And the tip of a finger touching a nose

I will put in my box . . .

A teddy with a thinking brain
A sip of water from the coldest ocean
And a talking calculator

I will put in my box . . .

The sound of a car in a traffic jam
The last blow from a whistle
And the first ray from a light

I will put in my box . . .

A cold, cold sun
A pig with a squeak and a
Guinea pig with an oink

My box is fashioned from gold and feathers
and one stained glass window
With magic fairy dust on the lid
And the smell of guinea pigs and rabbits in the corners
Its hinges are bits of steel from the ground.

I shall swim in my box
With the dolphins of the deep blue sea
Then wash ashore on a yellow beach
The colour of the sun.

Katie Hawes (8)
Stoke Hill Junior School

The Magic Box

(Based on 'Magic Box' by Kit Wright)

I will put in my box . . .
The run of river
The smell from the mouth of a shark
The tip of a finger touching a toe

I will put in my box . . .
A pencil with a headache
A sip of wine from a bottle
The jump from a dolphin

I will put in my box . . .
The sound of a tree collapsing
The last memory of my grandad's cancer
And the first ride in a sports car

I will put in my box . . .
A belly man and a pink moon
A mole up a tree
And a squirrel underground

My box is fashioned from colours and ribbon
With writing on the lid and light in the corners
Its hinges are the diamonds of London

I shall skate in my box
On the bluey-white ice of the freezing Atlantic
Then go on an adventure
Which is the colour of the bright sea.

Alex Morgan (8)
Stoke Hill Junior School

The Magic Box

(Based on 'Magic Box' by Kit Wright)

I will put in my box . . .
The first step of a baby
The swish of a chocolate milkshake
A first touch of the lips

I will put in my box . . .
The saltiest sip from the saltiest sea
A bogeyman with a rumbling belly
And a cat's fluffy fur

I will put in my box . . .
A rustle from the first leaf of spring
The last goal from Bobby Charlton
And the first bark from the mouth of a dog

I will put in my box . . .
A time-twisting clock
Chris Ronaldo
And Cristeno Taren

My box is fashioned from paper and plaster and brick
With wrestlers on the lid and footballs in the corners
The hinges are the skin of a snake.

I shall play football in my box
On the greatest pitch of Manchester United
And hold up the FA Premier League Cup
Against West Exe.

Callum Oakes (9)
Stoke Hill Junior School

The Magic Box

(Based on 'Magic Box' by Kit Wright)

I will put in my box . . .

The hard kick from a football player
The Eyore from a donkey's big mouth
The feeling of a finger touching your nose

I will put in my box . . .

A robotic donkey having a heart attack
A sip from the warmest hot chocolate
An oink from a massive pig

I will put in my box . . .

Sound of a wild crowd clapping
The last bright light that shone
The first loving kiss from my ancient auntie

I will put in my box . . .

A fish that can talk
A bear bellowing woof and a
Dog howling roar

My box is made from
Bright crystals and real diamonds
With the tiniest of footprints on the lid
And loving kisses in the corners.

I shall ice skate in my box
On a frozen lake in the coldest Antarctica
Then fall over and bruise my leg, the colour of mud.

Ellie Bassett (9)
Stoke Hill Junior School

The Magic Box

(Based on 'Magic Box' by Kit Wright)

I will put in my box . . .

The first step of a human,
The spots from a panther's skin,
And the first kiss of love.

I will put in my box . . .

A dog with a brain,
A sip of the cleanest water from the South Pole
And the roar from a small tiger

I will put in my box . . .

The cheer of a football crowd,
A man jumping off the moon on the edge of a spoon,
And the first rustle from the leaves of a tree

I will put in my box . . .

The moon with a face but made of cheese,
A guinea pig that goes oink,
And a pig that squeaks.

My box is fashioned from leaves, stars and enchanted ivy.
With vines on the lid and mysteries in the corners,
Its hinges are made from the petals of a rose.

I shall grow flowers in my box
In the enchanted garden,
Then stop just beside a rose,
The colour of lava.

Amanda Herring (9)
Stoke Hill Junior School

The Magic Box

(Based on 'Magic Box' by Kit Wright)

I will put in the box . . .
The swing of a monkey
A roar from the mouth of a tiger
The tip of a toe touching a piece of sand

I will put in the box . . .
A teddy with a human headache
A sip of water from Dawlish Sea
A trunk from an elephant

I will put in my box . . .
Three special wishes spoken in Spanish
The last hug from my mum
And the first hug from my nan

I will put in my box . . .
A pen that can sing and dance
A horse that oinks
And a pig that goes neigh

My box is fashioned from glass, gold and flowers
With silver feathers on the lid
And love in the corners

I shall swim in my box
In the bluest water of the Turkish ocean
Then wash ashore on a big yellow beach
The colour of the rainbow.

Jade Chapman (8)
Stoke Hill Junior School

The Magic Box

(Based on 'Magic Box' by Kit Wright)

I will put in my box . . .

The waggle of a chinchilla's tail
Fluffy fur from a chinchilla
A finger touching an earring

I will put in my box . . .

A stone man with a rotten brain
A sip of the darkest fruit juice from Africa
A leaping bark from the mouth of a dog

I will put in my box . . .

The sound of an erupting volcano
My last football match
The first howl from a dog

I will put in my box . . .

A flatfish with a lava body
A fish in a cage
A mouse in the sea

My box is fashioned from gold and ice and diamonds
With stars on the lid and lightning in the corners
Its hinges are the bent teeth of dinosaurs

I shall swim in my box in the bluest sea then float ashore
To a yellow sandy beach the colour of the brightest yellow sun.

Liam Wallace (9)
Stoke Hill Junior School

The Magic Box

(Based on 'Magic Box' by Kit Wright)

I will put in the box . . .

A swish around the world on a summer night
A sharp tooth from a dog
A wet tongue touching a foot.

I will put in the box . . .

A teddy bear with a wobbly nose
A sip of the wobbly blue sea
A sharp claw from a cat.

I will put in the box . . .

Two blue wishes spoken out from a teddy
The last clap from a grandma and
The first time a toddler cycles.

I will put in the box . . .

An electric dog full of magic
A monkey on a bike,
A girl up a tree.

My box is fashioned from ice and rare blue gold and glitter,
With hearts on the lid
And magic in the corners
There are no hinges
As the lid opens when I tap it with my hand.

I will run in my box
On the biggest land of the Earth,
Then I'll smell a rose
The colour of lavender.

Siân Bond (9)
Stoke Hill Junior School

The Magic Box

(Based on 'Magic Box' by Kit Wright)

I will put in the box . . .

A swish of the world
A famous cat making a sound
The claws from a ginger cat
A tongue touching the tip of the cup

I will put in the box . . .

A piece of grass with a wobbly belly
A sip from the greenest apple tree
And an electric donkey full of sugar

I will put in the box . . .

Two pink wishes spoken in Spanish
The last laugh from a clever boy
And the first jump from a monkey

I will put in the box . . .

The webbed feet from a little duck
A monkey with a trunk
And an elephant up a tree

My box is fashioned from glass and feathers and steel
With silver stones on the lid
And fairy dust in the corners
Its hinges are the gold from a rich pirate on a ship

I shall swim in my box
In the great blue water in Ibiza
Then dive to the greenest pond
The colour of the grass.

Mylie Champion (9)
Stoke Hill Junior School

The Magic Box

(Based on 'Magic Box' by Kit Wright)

I will put in the box . . .
The sound of laughter from a baby on its first day,
The magic from a pretty unicorn,
And the smooth touch of a petal in the sun.

I will put in the box . . .
The flowing blood of a robot's heart,
The sweet taste of hot chocolate in the morning,
And the ferocious attack of a hyena.

I will put in the box . . .
Five pink whispers of a friend spoken in French,
The snore of a daddy sleeping in bed,
And the memory of when Millie was born.

I will put in my box . . .
The 10th season and the seventh green sun,
A baby wearing a cape,
And a princess wearing a nappy.

My box is fashioned from gold decorated with sapphires and rubies.
The top of the lid is red with rubies,
And the bottom of the lid is blue with sapphires.

I shall fly in my box with Millie,
To see the princesses in Disneyland,
Then come home to my family,
With a happy smile on my face.

Keeley Cummings (9)
Stoke Hill Junior School

The Magic Box

(Based on 'Magic Box' by Kit Wright)

I will put in my box . . .
The sound of a hamster talking to me,
The fire of a phoenix after it's changed
And the touch of Tutankhamun's death mask.

I will put in my box . . .
The unaided walk of a puppet,
The taste of icy cold rain in the winter
And a game of chase played by gerbils.

I will put in my box . . .
Seven yellow songs sung in Gujarati,
The last smile of a grandma
And the first step of a toddler.

I will put in my box . . .
The 30th of February which means a seaweed moon,
A scaly mouse that breathes fire
And a fluffy dragon that eats cheese.

My box is fashioned from the leaves
Of the most adventurous jungle in the world,
With the scales of a dragon for hinges
And whispers in the corners.

I shall go on adventures in my box
To the fiercest storm in Zanzibar
And the wildest jungle,
Filled with animals.

Lianda Kearns (9)
Stoke Hill Junior School

Emotions

Romance
Love is a meaningful sunset-pink,
Tasting like your first sip of red wine.
It smells like the perfume of a perfect rose that is utterly divine,
Like the look of a cuddled up kitten and puppy
In a basket near the stove.
It sounds like the crunch of popcorn in a lovey-dovey movie
At the pictures,
And feels someone's soft breathing, their body warmth against you.
It also makes you feel dizzy.

Envy
Envy is peacock-green,
And tastes like steamed limes.
It smells like a hospital full of old sick people.
Envy looks like the teacher who got the wrong end of the stick
About the fight in the playground and you get the blame.
The sound is like the constant loud drums from a gig
That ring in your ears like bells.
And makes me feel sick, like being ill while everyone else
Is playing in the sun.

Dolores Carbonari (10)
The Maynard School

The Star

I once saw a star shining bright,
As I looked up into the dark night,
It was bright, small and gold,
With a glowing warmth I'd love to hold,
I felt a surge of power,
As I looked up at it hour after hour.

Jemima Luxton (11)
The Maynard School

A Ginger Cat

Fish eater
Meat killer
Hand scratcher
Food snacker
Cute purrer
Snug curler
Milk drinker
Water sinker
Treat lover
Sweet hugger
High climber
Short timer
Basket sleeper
Noisy creeper.

Kate Middleton (8)
The Maynard School

A Giant

Earth breaker
Ground shaker

Noisy sleeper
Food sneaker

Heavy prancer
Wild dancer.

Hope Laws (8)
The Maynard School

Monkeys Kennings

Banana muncher,
Branch swinger,
Animal teaser,
Friendly smiler,
Back picker,
Zoo entertainer,
Long leaper,
Mad squeaker!

Katie Browne   (11)
The Maynard School

War

Sword grabber
Heart jabber
Head basher
Body slasher
Bow seizer
King pleaser
Blood spiller
Death driller.

Jazmine Bailey   (10)
The Maynard School

Mr Body Bits

There was once a man called Body Bits
But alas! He had no skin
His heart went pump, it's a muscular lump
And his blood flowed round within.

The blood rushed down his arteries
Then coursed into his veins
And when it was time to sleep
The heart slowed down in ease.

The brain is the boss, but he gets very cross
Because none of the organs work well
They just hang around, making no sound
Until the brain rings a bell.

The brain sends messages down the spinal cord
Along through the nerves, racing like a sword.
The brain never switches off, it works all day long
And even when you're fast asleep, it's still going strong.

Like a Cyclops with one bulging eye
And this I tell you is no lie
His eye was oozing, squelching and weeping
And the pus and blood was endlessly seeping!

Then all of a sudden a vein burst!
I thought this was horrible enough, at first
It's getting really gruesome, I know
The shiver up my spine is starting to grow.

Mr Body Bits' lungs help him breathe
But they make him cough and they make him wheeze
When the snow comes, he starts to freeze
He gets all clogged up and starts to sneeze!

When he was young, the lungs looked like balloons
But now he is old, they look like prunes
Poor Mr Body Bits will die when they stop
And then sadly the air sacs will go pop!

Mr Body Bits was happily walking along
Until he drank some Coke
It made him burp, it made him slurp
Then it all went horribly wrong!

His kidneys got all muddled up
As the renal vein was not working
For on the inside, there was lurking
The lid of the Coke! Uh! Oh!

He googles and gurgles and takes one big bite
Slipping and sliding it goes out of sight
The stomach is busy while crushing away
Killing all bacteria while it hides away.

The small intestine is a very long tube
It carries away the left over food
The large intestine squeezes in haste
Until out through the rectum goes the waste!

Form Two (Year 5)
The Maynard School

Emotions

Loneliness
Loneliness is a dusky grey,
It tastes like stale burnt toast, black as can be,
The smell of loneliness is burning iron.
Loneliness looks like a never-ending black hole,
It sounds like an owl hooting at midnight.
Loneliness makes me feel haunted!

Joy
Joy is indigo-blue,
Joy tastes like trickling chocolate sauce.
The smell of joy is lush, fresh rushes by the river.
Joy looks like an outstretched lake
Surrounded by over-hanging trees,
It sounds like birds tweeting at dawn,
Joy excites me!

Alicia Boam (10)
The Maynard School

Thunder And Lightning

He stalks the skies
King of all eternity
Years of ruling but still never weakened
He claws and scratches
Breathing raggedly before lashing out
Arguing with his opposite
Who growls and rumbles, shouting awkwardly
They never stop
But bickering long and loud for all to see and hear
It flickers and burns then draws back guilty and ashamed
Waiting for his opposite to calm
And then all goes quiet
As the morning dawns, a fresh day.

Kathryn Sanders (11)
The Maynard School

Sunset

The amber sun drifts over the hills
Another day gone forever,
Lost, alone and deserted.

The golden sun starts to sink,
The past is behind it,
It will never be seen again.

The fading sun disappears,
Its time will come again,
But now the moon is here,
And is determined to capture the skies.

The moon dominates the heavens,
Glaring at the sun,
He is not exactly happy,
But has gained back his power.

Nancy Laws (11)
The Maynard School

Emotions

Love
Love is a perfect passionate candy pink.
And owns the taste of fluffy candyfloss.
It smells of a newly bloomed rose,
And looks like a light at the end of the tunnel.
It has the sound of rustling leaves,
Love fills me with happiness.

Disappointment
Disappointment is a deep dark blue.
It tastes of wrinkled prunes,
And smells like a musty rubbish dump.
It looks like an unlit cave,
And sounds like dripping water.
Disappointment makes me feel blue.

Lauren Talbot (9)
The Maynard School

Emotions

Jealousy
Jealousy is sea-green
It tastes like fire burning in your mouth
And smells like rotten eggs
It looks like a rubbish dump
And sounds like creaking doors in a haunted house
Jealousy is disgusting.

Relaxation
Relaxation is baby-pink
It tastes like an everlasting strawberry ice cream
And smells like freshly cut grass on a summer's day
Relaxation looks like fluffy newborn puppies
And sounds like new waves crashing against
The golden sand on the beach,
Relaxation feels like having a lie-in on a cold winter's morning.

Eleanor Peters (10)
The Maynard School

Emotions

Love
Love is soft, warm, pink and delicate,
It tastes like violet chocolates and spaghetti Bolognese,
Love smells like perfume, hot restaurants and crowded streets,
It looks like fluffy kittens and a cute boy opposite you,
Love sounds like birds twittering, a warm voice enclosing you
And the fire crackling.
Love feels like Christmas nights, someone's lips pressed against yours,
And a warm embracing body.

Jealousy
Jealousy is an ugly, emerald-green,
It tastes like flowers that have been diluted and made into demons,
Jealousy smells like a rotting, toxic wound,
It looks like a poisonous, writhing snake that bites and never lets go,
Jealousy sounds like a throbbing heart and unheard screaming,
It feels like drowning in cold hate and envy.

Anastasia Bruce-Jones (10)
The Maynard School

Revolting Rubbish Rhyme

I was in my bedroom one night,
I smelt a horrible pong,
So I went downstairs to see what it was,
And the smell got horribly strong.
I opened the door and stepped into the night,
And what I saw was a shocking sight!
Sitting around the garbage bin,
Was my old banana skin, a sweet wrapper and the biscuit tin
I heard the banana skin talk, I heard it say . . .
'So now can we get the garbage men to go away?'

Joanna Sanders (9)
The Maynard School

Emotions

Love
Love is ruby-red,
It tastes like hot chocolate sponge pudding,
And smells like the salty seawater on a beach,
Love looks like red roses on a warm day,
And sounds like a newborn kitten purring,
Love feels like a cuddle to keep you safe.

Hate
Hate is black,
It tastes like mouldy plums,
And smells like damp clouds above,
Hate looks like you are all alone,
And sounds like you're about to be squashed,
Hate feels like you don't have any friends in the world.

Amy Parnall (9)
The Maynard School

Emotions

Joy
Joy is a glowing sunshine-yellow,
It tastes like freshly picked, juicy strawberries,
And smells like new hay bales in a barn,
Joy looks like a newborn lamb skipping in a green meadow,
The hum of bees is the sound of joy,
Joy is amazing, so brilliant.

Sadness
Sadness is frosty blue,
And tastes like gone off milk,
It smells like leaking gas,
Sadness looks like an old cobwebby attic,
The sound is like a dripping tap,
Sadness feels cramped and small.

Rosalia Taylor (10)
The Maynard School

St George

Good aimer
Stick flamer
Amazing fighter
Fire lighter
Battle darer
Armour wearer
Horse rider
Arrow glider
Shield basher
Sword clasher
Dragon slayer
War player
Banquet eater
Non cheater.

Romilly Moran (7)
The Maynard School

A Dog

Face licker
Feet tickler
Fur shedder
Stick getter
Heavy sleeper
Lonely weeper
Eye shiner
Fire snoozer
Tail chaser
Friend maker.

Iona Mooney (8)
The Maynard School

A Princess

Joy bringer
Pretty singer
Little kisser
Jolly hisser
Beautiful sister
Ugly blister
Strange lover
Fat mother
Heart warmer
Naughty corner
Child spoiler
Wild runner
Real stunner.

Kate Timperley (8)
The Maynard School

Cat

Cute animal
Fluffy mammal
Rat hater
Mouse eater
Milk licker
Grass flicker
Skinny player
Smooth prancer
Soft trotter
Mice stopper.

Anne Lancaster (7)
The Maynard School

Word Kennings

Friend maker
Funny shaker
Good singer
Fantastic swimmer
Fast writer
Perfect dresser
Speedy runner
Lovely hummer.

Beth Salisbury (7)
The Maynard School

A Llama

Sand walker
Scruffy stalker
Dust flicker
Water licker

Fun player
Silent prayer
Fast trotter
Grass spotter.

Phoebe Taylor (7)
The Maynard School

Autumn Morning

Branch breaker
Ice shaker
Rain taker
Hedgehog waker
Fun bringer
Nice whistler
One flower
King bower.

Lucy Keeling (8)
The Maynard School

A Revolting Rubbish Rhyme

I carefully lift the top of the bin,
To drop the slimy banana skin in,
The horrible smell of last night's curry,
So awful, I dropped the lid in a hurry,
Our weekly rubbish collected by the refuse man,
Who throws it in his smelly, dirty refuse van,
He drives away to the huge dump site,
Where he empties all the rubbish, what a horrible sight!
That was the end of the rubbish story,
Which I thought was very gory.

Georgia Anthony (10)
The Maynard School

Emotions

Sadness
Sadness is the colour of icy blue frost
And tastes like bitter poison
It smells like a polluted world, that is not cared for,
Sadness is the sound of someone weeping alone
It makes me shiver and cry.

Naomi Martin (9)
The Maynard School

Anger

Anger is bright red.
It tastes like sour milk
And smells like burning orange flames.
It looks like hot bubbling lava
And sounds like beating war drums.
Anger frustrates me!

Molly Waring (10)
The Maynard School

Hate

Hate
Hate is a deep, cold, jet-black
It tastes like the juice of a bitter apple
And it smells like a cold, dark musty cellar
Hate looks like a big empty house with spiders' cobwebs
The sound of quietness, no voices
Stinging my eyes like a thousand bees.

Love
Love is the bright yellow, warm, sunny sky
The taste of fresh pears
The smell of a smoky bonfire
And the look of a sunflower blowing in the breeze
The sound of a deer jumping over the hedgerow
Love is my mother hugging me at night.

Isabelle Coventry (9)
The Maynard School

An Oviraptor

Egg stealer
Bad dealer

Strange chirper
Noisy slurper

Silly reader
Good leader

Plant hater
Excellent mater.

Sophie Bailey (7)
The Maynard School

A Leopard

Feline chaser
Spotty racer
Noiseless leaper
Motionless creeper
Longing fighter
Speedy runner
Water hater
Sulking drinker
Cunning thinker.

Sophie Mills (7)
The Maynard School

The Playground

The playground is an erupting volcano
Banging and hissing, burning and smoking
Sizzling past the climbing frame
Burning everything in its path

The playground is a dormant volcano
Still and smooth at dusk
Sliding towards dawn
The volcano begins to warm.

Callum Caine (10)
Willowbrook School

The Playground

The playground is a wild jungle
Screaming and thumping.
Crazy monkeys swing bar to bar.
Chatting to each other.

The playground is a deserted jungle
At the crack of dawn
In the dull light
All is peaceful and quiet
In the sleeping jungle.

Thomas Davenport (11)
Willowbrook School

The Playground

The playground is a tiger pouncing about hunting for food
Leaping around the climbing frame roaring.
Jumping up trees, rustling the leaves.
Stalking the birds in its jungle.

The playground is a patient tiger waiting for its prey.
Staring as it lies with grass rustling.

Hayden Burrows (10)
Willowbrook School

The Playground

The playground is a wild night jungle
That has parties every night.
It shouts and screams
Before the sign of dusk.

The party is over
Everything is quiet.
All the cake is eaten
And everyone has gone home.

Hanifa Nabizadeh (11)
Willowbrook School

The Playground

The playground is a wild jungle
Monkeys running and screaming
Lions and tigers climbing a tree
Gorillas telling them to get down

The playground is a jungle at rest
A blanket of leaves at dusk
With shadows of trees and lots of peace
The playground gently sleeps.

Lauren Winsor (10)
Willowbrook School

The Playground

The playground is a lively jungle,
Crowded with screaming monkeys,
Racing around on the twiggy ground,
Charging for the climbing frame.

At the crack of dawn the playground is still,
The weeping willow rustles,
The sun arrives up to the sky,
Birds begin to sing.

Amy Curley (10)
Willowbrook School

The Playground

The playground is an angry child
Shouting and screaming
Stomping off all over the place
A spoilt brat.

The playground is a sleepy child
Rustling the leaves
A gentle breeze brushing past the trees.

Zoe Gould (10)
Willowbrook School

The Playground

The playground is a screaming monkey swinging
Through the jungle screeching happily on the climbing frame
Leaving banana skins on the grass.

The playground is a curled up monkey
Asleep and silent
Its stomach is full, he rests
Monkey waits for early
Morning breakfast.

Joe Wakefield (11)
Willowbrook School

The Playground

The playground is a steaming, furious jungle,
Little animals crying for their mums.

Screaming and roaring on their backs
Will anyone help them?

The playground is a quiet jungle,
Lots of snoring and gentle roar, smooth,
Nothing to hear, just a gentle snore.

Jake Coles (10)
Willowbrook School

The Playground

The playground is a playful lion
Rearing and racing
He shakes his fur round and round
Proud and strong in his territory

The playground is a basking lion
Sleeping peacefully in the sun
He sharpens his nails all day
He cleans his fur at the crack of dawn.

Louise Vicary (10)
Willowbrook School

The Playground

The playground is a wild jungle
Screaming and thumping.
Crazy monkeys swing bar to bar
Chattering to each other.

At the crack of dawn
In dull light
All is peaceful and quiet
In the sleeping jungle.

Jai Coombes (11)
Willowbrook School

The Playground

The playground is a boxing kangaroo
Jumping through the wet grass
Skipping and getting his feet wet
Hopping all the way to the climbing frame

The playground is a tired kangaroo
Sleeping on the wet grass
Leant on the climbing frame
Closing his eyes slowly.

Nathan Henley (11)
Willowbrook School

Young Writers Information

We hope you have enjoyed reading this book - and that you will continue to enjoy it in the coming years.

If you like reading and writing poetry drop us a line, or give us a call, and we'll send you a free information pack.

Alternatively if you would like to order further copies of this book or any of our other titles, then please give us a call or log onto our website at www.youngwriters.co.uk

Young Writers Information
Remus House
Coltsfoot Drive
Peterborough
PE2 9JX

(01733) 890066